CW01080590

COLOR THERAPY

COLOR THERAPY

Healing With Color

by
R. B. Amber

ASI Publishers Inc., 127 Madison Avenue
New York, N.Y. 10016

2 3 4 5 6 7 8 9 10

Printed in the U.S.A. by
Noble Offset Printers Inc.
New York, N.Y. 10003

THIRD EDITION

Library of Congress Cataloging in Publication Data

Amber, R   B
  Color therapy.

  1. Color—Therapeutic Use.   I. Title.
RM840.A4   1980   615.8′31   80-18622
ISBN 0-88231-067-4

Contents

PART I—THEORY: PAST AND PRESENT

PART II—HOW TO HEAL WITH COLOR

INTRODUCTION

This book can be read in two ways.

For those interested in the theory and philosophy of Chromotherapy, Part I—Theory: Past and Present—should be read first, studied carefully, and related to the reader's philosophical background. There he will find the modern scientific theories enumerated, their agreements and their disagreements, together with the problems space medicine has posed for allopathic medicine, as well as a theoretical-philosophical consideration of color. This is the challenge that color healing presents today to the medical profession—a challenge inviting endless speculation.

For those interested in the immediate practice and pragmatic application of color therapy, Part II—How to Heal with Color—should be read first, for here the readers will not find any philosophic theories or speculations. In this section, a set of directives applying color to the dietary problem of man—How to Lose Weight and How to Gain Weight—is followed by an analysis of the properties and the healing powers of color. It ends with a list of the various diseases, the specific colors to be used in effecting cures, and the application of color to foods. Part II is specific and, at all times, practical.

Part I

Theory
Past and Present

CHAPTER 1

COLOR AND LIGHT: MODERN VIEWS

Colortheraphy or Chromotherapy is the science which uses different colors to change or maintain vibrations of the body to that frequency which signifies health, ease, and harmony. These color rays may be visible or invisible to the human eye, and they can be applied to the body either physically, through definite exposure to the light rays themselves, or mentally, through techniques of suggestion, visualization, or meditation.

Healing by means of color was probably the first type of therapy used by man because it was nature's own method and a natural device for keeping the organism in balance and rhythm. When man first walked the earth, the sun's rays fed him and kept him warm; the color of the flora and fauna accounted for his mood and temperament; the rhythm of the winds and the murmur of the seas rocked him to sleep. He may not have had the knowledge and the technical skills of modern man, but neither did he have the psychiatrogenic and iatrogenic diseases induced by the suggestions or the practices of the physician. Why? Because early man had the wisdom to live by nature's laws. Color is basic to any system of healing, whether or not the physician knows it.

Postulates Basic to Color Healing

1. All objects have characteristic frequencies of vibrations.
2. All organs have characteristic frequencies of vibrations in health.
3. Disease is altered function which is the natural response of the body to strain.[1] Altered function is nothing more than a change in frequency, the stepping-up or the lowering of a

---

1. The term strain is used, and not stress, which is Selye's terminology. Strain implies unnatural stress because it distorts. Stress is a natural, non-distorting function of the cell; without stress there would be no life in the cell.

3

vibration caused by a strainer—whether chemical, mechanical, or thermal. Germs are one of many hundreds of strainers. Therefore all diseases have characteristic frequencies of vibration.

4. The application of the right frequency—whether food, drugs etc.—will change altered function because the body has a tendency to return to its original pattern if given an opportunity.

5. Cells have selectivity taking the rays and vibrations as well as rejecting the rays/vibrations they do not need. If the cells lack color, which is another name for food, they begin to depolarize and change their frequency and therefore their pattern of growth.

6. The wrong color or the wrong type of food tends to change the frequency of the electro-magnetic field force of the cell, and this force interacts with the larger field force of the organ which, in turn, affects the system which then reacts upon the total field force of the body (typical chain reaction). This change leads to fatigue, and the degree of fatigue is the cause of exhaustion and death.

7. Color, being pure vibration, is the rational type of therapy for health and disease because it is in the right form, in the right place, at the right time.

Plight of Modern Allopathic Medicine

(Dichotomies Posed by the Fallacies of the Germ Theory and the Psycho-Somatic Compartmentalization of the Patient)

Today, Physicians know much about symptomology and disease, but less and less about cure. With all of the techniques available and with the information about bacteria—a formidable body of knowledge—more and more people are sick and the hospital is becoming the most popular type of architecture. Despite the pontifical air of the doctor, disease is increasing and fewer patients are getting well. The more ornate and technically equipped the hospital being built, the lower its percentage of cures. Could it be that orthodox medicine is so concerned with techniques and procedures for sterilization that its thinking has become sterile? Could it be that the philosophic basis of allopathic medicine rests on an inadequate premise wherein the germ theory has led research into a waste land and the people suffer and die needlessly?

The great bacteriologist of our time René Dubos stated that doctors were successful in treating patients long before anything was known about germs. These doctors had no knowledge of sulphur drugs[2] or antibiotics,[3] no vaccines, no serums for immunization. Yet, they were successful in their cures. Is it possible that the secret of their cures lay in a highly developed instinctive skill in treating the patient **as a whole man** coupled with a reliance upon their other intuitive awareness of the consciousness of the patient? Is is possible that the secret lay in not looking for one cause of a condition, as the modern physician does, and in treating just that one cause, but in treating the vibrations of **the entire man?** Or perhaps the answer may be found in another statement by René Dubos.

With regard to germs, Dubos observed that bacteria and viruses become dangerous only when the body's natural balance is disturbed. Otherwise, even the most virulent of these bacteria are harmless. It is interesting to note that it is practically impossible to infect volunteers picked at random with some supposedly highly infectious disease if the experimenters do not know how to upset the internal environment so as to produce the right conditions. Dubos is not the first nor will he be the last to point out the fallacy of the germ theory of disease and its inadequacies. Yet why does allopathic medicine go blindly marching down to its destruction with most of society dancing along? Dr. Oliver Wendell Holmes' statement made in 1860 holds true today. "I firmly believe that if the whole **materia medica** as it is now used could be sunk in the ocean it would be better for mankind, and all the worse for the fish."

---

2. Sulphur drugs kill bacteria by taking in sulphur and employing it in reaction which normally calls for a Vitamin, para-amino benzoic acid—PABA.
3. Penicillin inhibits the normal action of adensine triphosphate—ATP—which normally exists in all cells and serves as a battery to release the energy needed by the cell. ATP is essential for the normal action of the cell.

Are the sociologists correct when they say that man posses-ses a strong psychological reluctance to leave old pathways and permit new ideas to flourish; that there is a strong tendency for the In-Group in society to identify itself with the conventional standards to the exclusion of new ideas? Ideas that have grown conventional become inert, stagnant; they lose their electrical charge and acquire a dogma and a rigidity which can be changed only by evolution or revolution. Medical science today is tortured by this inflexibility; as long as it conforms to the values implicit in convention, it can and will find all the support and encouragement from the vested interests of its society and from the propaganda machines that feed these stereotypes into channels of public opinion.

Allopathic medicine, despite its research program and its dis-bursements of millions, has made only a slight contribution to the cure and prevention of disease. At present it has generated a large body of dogma, doctors who interpret, instead of priests, and mil-lions of sacrificial victims. The doctors are the pied pipers piping their dogma-tunes, the popular melodies of the wonder drugs, and the millions of sacrificial victims go dancing to their destruction.

Are the psychologists correct when they say that man's de-sire for something permanent may be related to the psychological urge to reduce anxiety or tension? This thinking has led its scien-tific adherents to stress the dual nature of the organism: the psyche versus the soma. It is much easier and much less frustrat-ing to compartmentalize the organism than to regard the being as a whole. Thus with the modern fetish for specialization, think of what complications might ensue in the practice of medicine if the non-Euclidean assumption were made: The whole man is greater than the sum of his individual parts — psyche and soma.

The psychologists, the psychiatrists, the clergy,[4] the sociologists, and even the police are now faced with treating disturbed individuals. Man has never before been treated on so

4. Unfortunately, most western religions condition the individual with a negative attitude that disease and suffering are a necessary part of life. The acceptance of this attitude inhibits the individual and results in wrong think-ing and disharmony. Color meditation and instructing the subconscious mind with the idea of health before going to sleep are indicated here.

many fronts by what may be conveniently termed the "mentalists". But in our society today, these people, as patients, have status, prestige, and the binding common language of psychoanalysis that admits them to the circle of the sacred elite. At any rate, modern psychiatry has made clear the distinctions separating the neurotic and the psychotic from the psychiatrist. The first builds castles in the air; the second lives in them; and the third collects the rent. But none of the three is concerned with vibration or color-healing.

Is the historian correct when he says that all of history is nothing more than a record of blaming somebody else who is outside the special group? In orthodox healing, if some thinker or independent chooses to wander from the Halls of Ivy, then the psychological forces that brought the Spanish Inquisition into being charge into action. If that inquisitive maverick is lucky, he will be labelled dreamer, faker, charlatan, or quack. The drug companies call the turn today.

This chapter discusses color and light as viewed by the modern scientists — and here the orthodox as well as the unorthodox will be included (the odd-ball scientist's heresy of today has the habit of becoming the conservatism of tomorrow). Further the contributions made to an analysis of color by philosophers, by educators, and by some occultists will be touched upon. Those who view color as a static force will be compared with those who interpret color as a dynamic force. Each one presents a theory which is a fragment of the role color plays in healing. But all the theories must be inter-related and reinterpenetrated to show their spinning interweavings. The different slanted views play their part in revealing man's response to light and color! Here one pieces together these various fragments chiseled and hammered by the philosopher, the scientist, the occultist, the psychologist, and the educator. The historical approach appraising the theories of color healing advocated in the past, thousands of years ago, by other cultures from the East will be treated in the second chapter: contributions to chromotherapy made by Egypt, India, China and Persia together with the forgotten lore of mythology — all of which will reveal a vast knowledge about light and color. These principles the modern scientists are beginning to re-discover and to utilise, but in many instances without any philosophic bases or tenable working premises.

The conventional scientist pooh pooh's the comparative historical research methodology that seeks to appraise the findings of the occultists or the teachings of the Indians and the Chinese. He is condescendingly content to leave this type of inquiry to his so-called "science" inferiors: the historian, the psychologist, the individual trained in the arts and in the humanities. He conveniently forgets or is totally unaware that the words **Open Sesame** of the story of Ali Baba, occult until recently, are now an every day occurrence. The opening of the cave by the magic words **Open Sesame** as a sound vibration is duplicated thousands of times each day in any large city where the electric eye is in operation. The occult of yesterday seems to become the scientific maxim or truism of today. This statement does not mean that everything labelled occult is accurate or sacred. Far from it! There is just as much nonsense in occultism as in the other disciplines. Mythology, occultism, philosophy, the scientific method — all are roads leading to knowledge. Knowledge for the sake of knowledge is useless, but knowledge properly used is wisdom.

In occult teachings, color, sound, and fragrance are the three basic remedies against human diseases. The method of healing is to create harmony and balance in the mind and body. Over-exposure to any one color or vibration can be corrected by using the complementary color or vibration. Any interference in the harmony of the body — whether from within or without, from an infection or lesion, from fright or wrong thinking — sets the forces of nature into action to heal.

These forces of action (static or dynamic) are important for an understanding of color therapy. Different theories have advanced different names for these centers of vibration, and mention is made, in passing, of only six views (a more complete discussion is found in the author's book on **Nu Reflex Therapy**).

1. H. Selye, in his work on endocrinology, voiced a theory for diseases which emphasized the General Adaptation Syn-

drome (Stress Theory). The author observes that the endocrine system and the chakras are the same for physiological purposes. While Selye did not mention color, the Hindus and the occultists do. Each endocrine organ has its own color, can be treated by color to remove the stress syndrome, and plays a role in the stress syndrome.

2.   H.H. Bergson, in his book, calls it **Elan Vital.**
3.   F.M. Alexander, in his work, calls it **Primary Control** and the controlling centre is the Atlantoid-Occipital region.[5]
4.   E. Coue calls it **Auto-suggestion.**
5.   S. Freud calls it **Libido,** and the **subconscious** is considered the controlling centre.
6.   New Thought teachings and Theosophy — Western philosophies that are partially derived from the Hindu and partially from Quimby — believe that all manifestation is produced by the Universal Mind or Cosmic Consciousness. The greater the harmony between the Universal Mind and the individual mind, the more rapid the healing. Mind and matter are interrelated, and a change in one is accompanied by a change in the other. All healing depends on the mental attitude of the individual. Here is seen a substitution of thought, a very powerful vibration, for color: one vibration for another (it is the author's opinion that thought has color).

What is important to grasp from these six is that despite the names assigned to these forces of action, treatment is aimed at the total man; color with its use of light and sound is significant in keeping man healthy and in treating his ills so that he functions in harmony and balance (Cannon calls this state Homeostasis).

The reader is simply reminded

1.   That in mental institutions color and music **today are becoming a necessary part of therapy** (Vibration).
2.   That backward and retarded children learn faster in yellow colored rooms (Color).

5. This is the author's explanation of the location of the centre of Primary Control.

3. That **music is more effective** than psycho-analysis **in reaching the emotionally disturbed** (Vibration).

But one trained in what is called "spiritual research" finds these three listings elementary. To him, light is positive and color negative. Further, he believes that color and sound are aspects of vibration and are inter-changeable, for he accepted as a fact that man could go from one vibration to another long before color was made audible to the ear by the **Aurotone,** an instrument that reproduces sound in color and where each color vibration is transferred to a sound equivalent. The seven colors of the spectrum are attuned to the seven tones of the musical scale; the three primary colors compose the first chord of music. On the Auratone, Note C vibrates to the color red;

Note E vibrates to the color yellow;
Note G vibrates to the color blue.

It may be observed that color and music play a vital part in the evolution of the subtle bodies of man. The seven visible colors of the spectrum and the seven notes of the scale have their effects on the seven subtle bodies which, according to Indian philosophy, surround and interpenetrate the physical body; the magnetic and electrical radiations from these bodies compose the aura. But the seven colors of the spectrum and the seven notes of the scale affect the seven bodies, especially on the physical, emotional, mental and psychic planes. The purer the color, the finer the tones, the greater is the effect on the body (Goethe, who was a student of occult philosophy, said that the vibrations of the white light are stepped down to meet the needs of the evolution of the earth).

The scientists all agree that the body is composed of air, water, minerals, and heat or warmth, but they do not all agree that the body also has a soul, the substance of which is color. But in experiments, color has become a characteristic of the body that can be measured—whether or not one believes in the presence of the soul. Color is an aspect of the body; to those who believe in the soul, it may be said that color is as necessary to the soul as air is to the body.

How does color become a vital part of man's health? It may be said, without any disagreement, that mental illness sometimes seems to be due to physical ailments which, in turn, are due to social ills over which the individual has no control. A number of research studies has even suggested that Cancer and Tuberculosis are sociological diseases. Whether or not one wishes to go this far in his agreement, one can safely conclude that some individuals cannot adjust to their environment. Even religion seems to offer them little help, for religion has come to signify morality based on an unattainable or scarcely to be attained ideal. Thus there is a conflict between the demands of daily living and the reachings out for an ideal, for a mode of belief and confidence that has no relationship to syllogistic reasoning. Man lives in two worlds, not as Matthew Arnold said — "one dead and the other struggling to be born" — but in a world of two types of knowledge and awareness. On one he struggles with the imperious demands of logical thought, common sense, reality subject to training and on which education builds information; but in the other, he lets flow into his consciousness or uncovers in his awareness that intuitive world which has no relationship to reason, in which imagination and emotion play a significant role, and to which he cannot add a jot or a tittle by formal training or education. He can only uncover it and let it flow or else throttle it or drown it **if he can.**

Without a bridge between these two worlds — the inner and the outer-man has no guide for daily living. **COLOR IS THAT BRIDGE**

When the nitrogen cycle is studied, the classic texts neglect to account for the role of color. Without color, the nitrogen cycle cannot work. Similarly with the analysis of a drop of water. The students study Newton's theory of light — as reflected through a lens — but they do not apply his theory to a water globule as it is found in nature with its surround either inside or outside the body. Thus the students do not comprehend the role of color/vibration in life as seen in a drop of water.

The Nitrogen Cycle — Color Explanation

Oxygen is taken from the atmosphere by the animal kingdom, unites in the body with carbon and is exhaled mainly as carbon dioxide. The carbon dioxide is absorbed by the plants through the action of the red and yellow rays. The plant breaking down the carbon dioxide then utilizes the carbon for growth and returns the oxygen to the air. By this cycle between the animal and vegetable kingdom, the balance of carbonic acid and free oxygen (which is about 20 per cent of the atmosphere) is maintained. The plants yield oxygen needed by animals who in turn give out carbon dioxide required by the plants.

Nitrogen is taken up by the plant in the form of ammonia, nitrates or nitrites, and these are converted into vegetable protein by the action of violet and indigo rays. This vegetable protein is utilized by the animal kingdom and is broken down into amino acids, urea, uric acid and other compounds. The urea and uric acid that decompose rapidly outside the organism yield ammonia which the plant needs.

Potassium, sodium, calcium, magnesium and iron unite with phosphorous, sulphur, chlorine, flourine, silicon, and oxygen to form the twelve tissue salts necessary for health. These salts — dissolved in sap — all enter the vegetable kingdom from the earth; by their proportion, the tissue salts determine the species of plants. These salts unite under the influence of the rays of all colors with the organic products to become the plant, vegetable, fruit, etc. that the animal utilizes as food.

Since carbonic acid is the primary compound which the plant must absorb from the atmosphere, it is highly significant that the color of most plant surfaces exposed to the air is green, for a green surface absorbs the maximum amount of red — the color ray complementary to green. It is the red ray which as the main factor in the absorption of carbonic acid gives the plant the carbon it needs for growth and releases pure oxygen in the atmosphere for reuse by the animal kingdom.

Drop of water: Spectroscopic Analysis

Each drop of water breaks up light into the seven visible colors which spread into and throughout the drop; red runs around the circumference, violet sits in the centre; and all the intermediate colors present themselves in their ordered sequence. Life-form patterns of physical substances always take their shape in the red or orange portion of the drop. In contrast fixed patterns resulting from mental concentration of abstract subjects always form in the portion of the drop colored by light rays more rapid than red or orange; namely, in the yellow, green, and blue. Patterns resulting from concentration of spiritual subjects always form in the indigo and violet, or central, portion of the drop.

Dr. Charles W. Littlefield discovered that if minerals were moistened and the water permitted to evaporate, a vital force appeared in the mineral particles having the characteristics of the various tissues of the body. Newton's laws cannot explain Littlefield's discovery. In the presence of a mineral salt solution, when a person concentrates upon an idea, these mineral particles form a picture and duplicate the image as the person had visualized it. This thought energy has physical manifestations which can be received **only in the presence of light of the right color,** as has been demonstrated by Philip Cancellor, inventor of this extraordinary technique of Thought Photography.

Ghadiali: Theory on Nature of Matter

Ghadiali, whose work in color healing is basic, related color and vibration to the physiology of the body. He observed that there are no pure elements; the elements themselves are compounds. Atomic physics substantiates this view. No element has a single or pure spectrum. Matter disintegrates, and all matter radiates as a result of this disintegration; for example, each metal has an odor of its own. Odor is a stimulation of the olfactory tract by particles in the air. If the metal were not disintegrating, it would be unable to issue an odor (L. E. Eeman's experiments found radiation from matter could be conducted by wires to affect the human organism). Light is thus a function of the disintegration of matter.

Ghadiali continued with stating that the sun gives no light, but the combustion gives off energies. These energies are converted into light by friction as they pass through the density of the earth's atmosphere. Color is nothing but a divisional part of light, a narrow portion of the vibratory range of the forty-ninth vibration.

Sound, heat, light, magnetism are all the same energy, differing only in frequency of vibration and the medium of conduction. All known energies are composed of oscillatory frequencies in different media of transportation, and all life, as contrasted to the matter in which life manifests itself, is composed of energies. Therefore it is easy to understand how the administration of light reinforces the life energies of the human body (it is the author's opinion that the ministry of the future will find its substance in light).

Physics of Light

Static school: Newton's Theory Luminous Energy Theory

Wave Theory and Quantum Theory

Maxwell's Electromagnetic Theory

The corpuscular, emission, or Newtonian theory of light — consisting of material particles or corpuscles sent off in all directions from luminous bodies — as stated in its original form has long been abandoned.

According to the undulatory or wave theory, light is transmitted from luminous bodies to the eye and other objects by an undulatory or vibrational movement. The velocity of this transmission is about 186,300 miles a second and the vibrations of the ether are transverse to the direction of propagation of the wave motion. The waves vary in length from 3.85 to 7.60 ten-thousandths of a millimeter, approximately. The color invoked when the energy impinges on the retina varies in a complex way with the wave length, the amplitude of vibration, and various other factors and conditions. Waves of a similar character whose length falls above or below the limits mentioned are not perceptible to the average eye under normal conditions. Those between 3.85 and 1.0 ten-thousandths of a millimeter constitute ultraviolet light and are manifested by their photographic or other chemical action. Those exceeding 7.60 ten-thousandths in length are the infra-red waves and are detected by their thermal effects.

The electromagnetic theory of light, originated with Maxwell, holds that these waves, including those of light proper, are the same in kind as those by which electromagnetic oscillations are propagated through the ether and that it is an electromagnetic phenomenon. The most important phenomena of light are reflection, refraction, dispersion, interference, and polarization.

The present theory of luminous energy is far removed from Newton's conception. Today luminous energy is described as radiant energy which by its action upon the organs of vision, enables them to perform their function of sight.[6] According to modern theory, light both visible and invisible consists of quanta of energy which move as guided by waves, the statistical behavior of the quanta being determined by the fact that their energy at any point is on the average equal to the intensity of the wave system at that point.

Wave and Quantum Theories:[7] Science is baffled by the strange behavior of this mysterious medium called light. At present, scientists offer the **Wave** and the **Quantum** theories, but neither one individually nor both combined explain fully the phenomenon of light. It is becoming more and more apparent that both theories are inadequate even if both are combined to explain the objective and the subjective aspects of light.

How does physics provide man with explanations presumably indisputable? To the physicist, white light passing through a

---

6. Ultra-violet light or infra-red light, which at present is incapable of appreciably affecting the average normal retina, is radiant energy or acts like it.

7. Quanta are made up of discontinuous pulses which move in one direction slowly from West to East. The wave is a continuous movement rapidly going in the same direction (North or South or East or West).

prism becomes visible as red, orange, yellow, green blue, indigo, and violet. Beyond the visible spectrum are the red or infra-red rays on one end — considered heat rays — and on the other end are the ultra-violet rays. The wave lengths vary from that of the red (.000256 of an inch) to that of the violet (.0000174 of an inch). The physical eye perceives only the colors that fall on or between these wave lengths.

The invisible colors with longer or shorter wave lengths also affect the organism, as is seen from x-rays and supersonic waves. The important fact in color therapy is that each color has its own wave length and its own frequency. Color arises under certain conditions of interaction of radiant energy and matter. This interaction results in the absorption of certain wave lengths and the reflection of others. An object that appears black is one that has absorbed completely all the radiant energy of all frequencies. The object that appears white is the one that reflects all wave lengths. When an object absorbs definite portions of the spectrum and reflects others, it has color. A red object is one that has absorbed the blue region of the spectrum and reflects red. This selective absorption of light is the physical basis of color. The absorption of light is thought to be due to the jumping of an electron from one orbit to another or jumping on to a different energy level.

Dynamic School

Page	The Spiral
Psychologists, Physiologists	Lakhovsky
Chemistry of Color	Reich
Steiner, Simpson	Bergson
Goethe, Lehr	De La Warr
Experiments—	Radionics
Flammarion, Trinder	Burr and Northrop
Reiser	Biotonics
Author's Theory of Tumors	Ayurveda—Doshas

Professor Calvin S. Page disagrees with these interpretations made by the "static" physicists. He states that color is formed not only by waves, but also by their varieties of velocity. To him, colors are not produced by the absorption of some of the rays and the reflection of the others, as is the accepted theory, but are produced because all the light appearing as a certain color is altered in velocity. This is a good explanation for the healing properties of colors and their vibrations.

The psychologists and the physiologists provide this currently popular theory of color vision: There are three sets of color-sensitive nerves in the eye: yellow, blue and red. White light stimulates all of the three sets of color-sensitive nerves equally. If a stimulus is weaker or lacking to one or more sets of nerves, it produces color sensation. When one set of color-sensitive nerves is exhausted, the individual will be color blind in that primary color and hypersensitive to the others. If two sets of nerves are not functioning, the individual sees everything in one color— monochromic.

A further explanation of color must treat of chemical changes. It is well-known that the colors of chemical solutions have definite relations to their chemical composition. Any desired color can be produced by changing the structural formula to conform to the absorption area of the visible spectrum desired. A red solution is obtained by filtering out the green rays. Then the complementary color of the shade that is absorbed appears. This fact is the result of electronic behaviour.

Steiner is regarded as a scientist by some people, as an educator by others, as an occultist by a third set, as a philosopher by a fourth, and as a religious leader by a fifth group. The concern here is what Steiner said about color to unlock the door to healing. He was far in advance of the followers of the classical physical school who fragmentized color in terms of its physical properties, for he developed an educational system and a way of life based on color and rhythm. One may visit the schools set up in New York and elsewhere throughout the world to see his theory put into practice: color as an inseparable part of the curriculum affecting every phase of the individual's life.

Steiner, like Goethe, built up a physical science of color including that seen by the naked eye and that experienced subjectively. He went a step further, however, and taught how to understand color through the feelings and how to raise this perception. Color he divided into two categories: those that have lustre (red, blue, and yellow) and those that have image (green, white, black, and peach-blossom). The lustre colors have activity, and the image colors have form. Green was defined as the image of life; peach-blossom or flesh-color, the image of the soul; white, the image of the spirit; black, the image of lifelessness. Through these images of life, soul, spirit and death, the border land of sense perception is reached. Color is created by a light shining in the darkness.

Steiner maintained that sickness nearly always indicates a rift between the earthly consciousness and higher perception. An illness is often accompanied by a sense of darkness and depression; these vibrations can affect those around the sick person, and the healer must be strong enough to break through this psychic darkness.[8]

Steiner further observed that the soul always lives in color between light and darkness and man also lives in feeling between thought and will. Man is an air-being, inhaling and exhaling rhythmically; and he is also a light-being unfolding in the light of thought and thinking.[9] Thinking is living in light, and will is unconscious. Man can understand himself only as a soul germinating in the future enclosed in the past. "Light shines out of the east; darkness leads into the future. In Will is revealed the continually beginning, the continually germinating world."

The balance between thinking and will, said Steiner, is maintained through feeling. In the same way, the balance in the physical body is maintained between the head system and the metabolic or limb system through the rhythmic interplay of breathing and blood circulation. Health is a mobile balance be-

---

8. It is the author's opinion that if the healer does not break through this psychic manifestation, he fails the patient. He will discover that the effective methods, in addition to color, are mind over mind, suggestion, and autosuggestion.

9. Compare this theory with the opinion of Reiser that man lives in a water-medium.

tween two opposing forces. The head and nerve force are continually destroying nerve substances during consciousness. Too much activity in the mind in childhood deprives the limbs of development. It may produce an intellect without imagination and feeling; this in later life causes Sclerosis. Art in education is a corrective for these conditions.

Substance, according to Steiner, is continually built up by the metabolic activity. Too much of such activity produces sluggish thinking, bodily corpulence, and false growth, as in tumors. A correcting for this condition is also development in the arts. The middle man is the healer of the other two systems, the breath and blood system which is midway between the digestive and head system. It balances the polarities of the head and metabolism. Illnesses affecting breathing, such as asthma and hysteria, can be helped through the arts, color, music, rhythmic movement and rhythmic occupations — such as color weaving, speech, or rhythmic breathing.

Steiner regarded health as a mobile condition in which all these had to find and to keep their balance. The soul must balance between head and metabolism, thinking and will, light and darkness, past and future. Out of illness may come a new consciousness that re-establishes its balance in health. Life radiates color.

Other views, agreeing with and yet different from Steiner's, will be briefly mentioned. The scientist explains color from a mechanistic or material point of view; the physicist, from his technical view; the vitalist, from his religious view; some philosophers, from their view of color as a creative process continually going on in an interplay between light and darkness, between the positive and negative forces of life, or, as the Chinese phrase it, between the Yin and the Yang; still other philosophers, from a combined scientific and metaphysical view, see color as the healing reconciliation of opposing forces. If there be an imbalance in either direction — too great a materiality or too great a spirituality — ill health will result. Thus one may assume from these various theoreticians that color therapy can be applied on the physical, psychological, and spiritual level. Because color is perceptual, it influences both the physical and the higher senses and can heal the physical and the higher consciousness. Each specialist presents one aspect of color or one scale and one or more vibrations of consciousness. No one has quite Steiner's insight into the total functioning of color.

But one must return from the excursion of the mind to the problem of light.

In a direct consideration of healing with light, mention must be made of E. Brooke Simpson. His **New Light on the Eyes** shows how he successfully treated cataracts by the application of appropriate beams of light. Eyes, he said, need the energy of light to sustain their activity, just as the body needs food to keep it alive. Colors have a therapeutic value which is particularly potent when applied to the eyes. The visible rays of light are a natural medicine for an organ which functions by light.

The idea that light is connected with the process of mind is comparatively new in our culture, though ancient to others. Light through color may be regarded as an expression of expanding human awareness of itself and the cosmos. It is the connecting link between consciousness and pattern, a cosmic attribute joining the mental processes of the human being with cosmic functions. Light provides the means for a continuity of process between the organic entity and its environment at the non-material level. It is not by chance that the word **enlightenment** is used to denote a developing knowledge of cosmic meaning and an identity with it. Simply stated, **Light Determines Pattern.**

In the case of the growing plant can be seen a direct relationship between light and the emergence of pattern. A plant placed in darkness will strive toward the light. It will become deformed if necessary in what seems a purposeful attempt to reach the light. Biologists will say that this is heliotropism. The plant needs sunlight to bring about chemical processes by which it grows. This fact in the author's opinion is not an explanation, but merely an observation. In other words, says the author, light is dynamic, assisting the life forces within the plant to fulfill their function and to create growth in the form nature requires of them. Kept in darkness, it will languish; its form will not be true to type. Psychologically, the plant is neurotic (see Nitrogen Cycle).

To Goethe, color had a different view when he said, "The eye forms itself in order that the light from within may meet the light from without." He was one of the first to disagree with what is today the Newtonian theory of light maintained by orthodox scientists. Dr. Ernest Lehr, in his **Man or Matter,** deals with Goethe's views on light and color. Is it possible that Goethe refused to accept Newton's static interpretation because from his work in the occult, Goethe may have become familiar with color and its properties as explained by the Easterners as well as by the ancient Egyptians and as illustrated in the sacred steps of the Pyramids of Chaldea? In any case, whatever the reason for his rejecting the Newtonian theory, one must consider Lehr's suggestion that color is the result of two different regions of illumination. Here Lehr differs from the Gestaltists with their use of the figure-ground relationship. Both are using different tools to explain the same phenomenon.

Lehr observed these facts: Since all the processes of nature are functions of polar opposites in the polarity of light and darkness, Goethe stressed not light and its absence, but a dynamic[10] condition in which both are functions. This fact of interpretation means that colors are dynamic conditions caused by the interplay of light and darkness and that they therefore have secondary polarities. When one looks through a prism, a white wall will appear white. The only place where a band of color will appear is at the boundary where light meets darkness — in Gestaltist terminology giving figure and ground. It is at this point that the functioning of polarity comes into play and a dynamic condition ensues, which results in the phenomenon of color. It is also found that:

1. The colors differ according to the position of light and darkness in relation to the base of the prism.
2. The warm colors are seen — red to yellow.

10. Modern Gestaltists accept this viewpoint whether they realize it or not.

3. Where the relationship is reversed, the cold colors blue to violet appear.
4. To complete the spectrum, it is necessary to bring the two ranges of color together until they merge.
5. If they be merged by the enclosing of a narrow band of light between the two areas of darkness so that yellow meets blue, then green appears.
6. But if they merge by the insertion of a dark band in a field of light, a new spectrum appears and a color like peach-blossom or skin-color appears instead of green (recall Steiner's classification).

Lehr suggests that the rainbow is a color phenomenon on a **boundary** in the sky between two space regions of different illumination. "When we see a rainbow, what we are really looking at is the edge of an image of the sun disc caught and reflected owing to favourable conditions in the atmosphere." His observation would explain the supposition that light does not travel from the sun to the earth, but is an effect triggered off in the atmosphere by certain radiations. Obviously then, some boundary would exist in the upper atmosphere between light and darkness.

This view of a possible boundary is particularly interesting in the light of experiments conducted by Miss Turnbull of Bridgeport, England, and Philip Chancellor of Mexico. Miss Turnbull has taken photographs of planets with an ordinary camera and without the use of a telescope. According to classical physicists, this could not be done (she took pictures of reflected images in the atmosphere). Philip Chancellor took thought pictures in some cases without a camera and in other cases with a camera and in the absence of visible light. Here too the classical physicist said it could not be done. Littlefield's explanation is basic, and perhaps one is reminded of the story of the bee who, according to physicists, could not fly. The bee unable to read kept on flying.

These experiments by Chancellor of Mexico can be duplicated by anyone, but the theoreticians in physics cannot explain these manifestations according to orthodox theories. Physics tries to present a logical picture of light as a radiation, with white light, a combination of all other colors, and with darkness, an absence of light. This orthodox theory makes it difficult (1) to discriminate accurately in the act of seeing between the objective and the subjective or (2) to see that the scientific method can easily result in false conclusions if and when the observations are based on methods derived from an incomplete analysis[11] of what light really is. In the final analysis, the study of light involves more than the phenomenon of seeing.

A number of experts hold the view that the eye sends out a beam of energy itself which is of the nature of light and by which perception takes place. When any apparent contradiction to optical theory takes place, then the scientific explanation is that it is an illusion. Lehr gives the explanation of a green object illuminated by a green light which then appears to be black. According to the accepted orthodox theory, light reflected from any surface is that which strikes the eye. A white object reflects all the light, and white is seen. If an object is to be seen as green in a white light, all other colors, according to the theory, are absorbed and only green is reflected. If only a red light is used, then it is all absorbed, and no light is reflected. If blackness is an absence of light, then the object not only appears black, but also is black. On the other hand, if a green light is used and reflected, the object appears white. Since only the frequency which produces green can strike the eye in this particular case, the question should be asked, why does not the eye register green? This question is answered with, "It is an optical illusion." In other words, the eye does not see properly. Let this principle be applied to plants.

In an orthodox classical experiment, a plant grown in green light should not absorb any light and this plant should therefore become deformed or die. Are the physicists correct? Two experimenters may be cited, for their findings run contrary to the views of the physicists: Flammarion and Trinder.

M. Camille Flammarion found that plants and animals were affected by light. Lettuce grown under red glass grew four times

---

11. What is called darkness may contain rays of light invisible to the naked eye at the present stage of man's development. Light is more than sight.

as quickly as in sun light, and it would shoot up to great heights, like a bean stalk. Under green glass it was taller than under sunlight (the orthodox theory says the plant should die or be deformed). Under blue glass, its growth was insignificant. Various plants subjected to different colored glass gave diverse results: for example, Indian corn under white light grew to twenty-five inches; under red, to eighteen inches. Beans flourished under white and red light, but died under green and blue light (the orthodox theory holds true here only for beans).

H. Trinder in his experiments found that metals have an affinity for certain colors; for example, tin had an affinity for white and iron for red. He stated too that he could get reactions in complete darkness. But he had some results that he could not explain. Some reactions in darkness were identical with those obtained in light, but others, for some unknown reason, were reversed. Obviously, for certain substances, when no visible light remained or when they remained in darkness, the effect of color was not extinguished. In such cases, this traditional scientific explanation **is not valid:** namely, that light becomes invisible only when it passes beyond a certain frequency band and that color is visible because it exists within a frequency band that is capable of affecting the optic nerve.

The author wishes to make this observation: A blow on the jaw makes the individual see stars or light. The explanation that the optic nerve is irritated and consequently produces light is begging the question. Where did the light come from in the first place? Some sort of light must be present in nerve conduction just as every activity of protoplasm is accompanied by an electric current. Color may be visible because it has a certain frequency, but in addition to that quality, it has others that are not normally observable and that are not explained by orthodox theory. All that is known at present is that under certain conditions, light does affect the optic nerve and light has other properties that affect the organism, but about which nothing or very little is known.

The orthodox scientist will disagree with Oliver L. Reiser whose **Alchemy of Light and Color** uses the scientific method with a philosophical-metaphysical slant when he considers the principles and the effects of color on the human organism. Reiser affirms that all living organisms on the physical plane are preponderantly water-oriented and water has the property of accelerating all kinds of chemical reactions. Carbon forms the building blocks of living matter because it has the power to form complex substances necessary for life, like proteins and carbohydrates. The carbon compounds are especially "optically active"; that is, they can rotate the plane of polarization of a beam of light passing through them, turning it either to the left or the right. Here can be seen a strong bond between color production and "optically active" carbon compounds. Living matter also contains lipins or fats insoluble in water and very necessary to life. These fats behave in a manner that can be duplicated by linseed oil, and there is a curious resemblance between linseed oil and protoplasmic respiration. Linseed oil takes in oxygen and gives off carbon dioxide, just as the cell does. Ultra-violet light accelerates this respiration in linseed oil just as it does in protoplasm. The reaction begins slowly and then speeds up. The intensity of the response is totally out of proportion to the intensity of the external stimulus.

Reiser then adds that color-tone or hue depends on 1) wave length, 2) light-tone, 3) tint, 4) brightness or luminosity (which is correlated with the energy of the stimulus or the amplitude of the wave), and 5) saturation or chroma (which depends on the mixture of short and long wave lengths). All these five determine the visual color experience. He then goes on to say that every theory of vision involves a theory of the chemical process on the retina and implies a theory of nerve conduction.

Toland suggests that pulse frequency is responsible for the cortical processes underlying brilliance of color. The hue may depend on the nerve arrangement tuned to a particular wave length, such as red, etc. Some sort of light is present in nerve conduction, just as every activity of protoplasm is accompanied by an electrical current. He further explains that in a dark room, a band of red light will be seen to have projecting from its side reddish-blue arcs. When the eyes are closed, a true after-image of this can be obtained. Nerve fibres when stimulated give off radiation. What one is really seeing is his own nerve currents. Carbon dioxide is given off by the unexcited nerve, and light may also be given off by the unexcited nerve. This light thrown or given off by the unexcited nerve Reiser calls consciousness.

If one were to imagine himself to be inside the molecules or atoms which are absorbing light, he would see the complementary color which someone outside the molecule would see as reflected light. In this sense, the internal universe of consciousness is the external universe turned outside in — like the functioning of a camera — and the internal world turned inside out. Life is literally a process of oxidation. Each nerve cell is a fire with its own fuel. Consciousness is a synthesis of many little glowings that depend on cerebral oxidation. Reiser further affirms that the consciousness of color somehow duplicates the physical conditions of color.

The nerve cell is a generator as well as transmitter. Both processes involve the breaking down and the restructuring as well as the resynthesizing of a long chain of carbon compounds. The kind of carbon compounds of which a cell is made is an expression of the way it functioned in the past. This fact suggests a relation between color and the structure of the brain. Hereditary modes of responses are usually explained as being the expression of "...innate pathways of low resistance or an inherited synchronism between nerve cells and muscle cells."

Is Reiser in his analysis really talking of polarization without being aware of it?

It is the author's belief, in answer to Reiser's observations, that

1. Although a compound may have the same formula, it may be poisonous in one case and non-poisonous in another case, depending on whether the plane of polarization is right or left.
2. This fact holds true for the orthodox theory.

According to Sir Lawrence Bragg, Nobel Prize winner, life on this planet can be described as oriented to the right, and man is like a "right-handed cork-screw."[12] Any "left-handed cork-screw" orientation would be poisonous to him: for example, should man land on Mars and find that the people there are oriented as "left-handed cork-screws", their food would be poisonous to earth-man (here the spiral theory could be used to devise a fascinating series of speculations).

Evidence now shows that the inherited modes of responses are due to something permanent about or in the cell, such as its molecular or electrical structure. This generalization may account for the fact that pathology is the exception, not the rule. Because of their permanent structure, cells tend to remain or to return to normal if given the opportunity.

Author's Theory for the Origin of Tumors and Mutations and His Discovery of the Law of Evolutionary Redundancy

If the repetition of a stimulus can alter cell structure, the so-called innate tendencies can be modified. Repeated stimulation compels the alteration of chemical structure and transfer of function. This fact has been proved indisputably by A.D. Speransky.[13]

The author theorizes that this manifestation of cellular alteration and modification can be used to explain tumors and mutations. If a strainer causes imbalance and if it is not removed so that the cell structure is altered, the environmental factors for the growth of the tumor are excellent and its surgical removal is just treating symptoms. This surgery becomes a delaying action, the process continues, and the organism dies.

If the strainer is removed, the organism tends to return to normal.

If the strainer is not removed, the organism sets up a collateral or secondary pathway. Here again the author's theory is that the organ to set up the collateral or secondary pathway continues with its own functions as well as takes on the functions of

---

12. See section on Chakras.
13. See his book, **A Basis for the Theory of Medicine.**

the first organ, now partially or completely out of commission. This process is a throwback in the evolutionary process before the specialization of the cell had evolved. In reality the cell is returning to its previous pathway.

The author terms this process of self-repair-emergency-retreat the law of Evolutionary Redundancy. The body, unlike the automobile, repairs itself; it is its own mechanic. The emergency system of the body in responding to strain or danger allows or forces the cell to return to its past, preceding evolutionary cellular stage where and when it could successfully perform all the functions required for living. The second organ does its own work and the work of the organ it has been called upon to help because of the inter-relationship of system and systems. It simply calls on its experience of the past. If the stimulus causes permanent alteration of the chemical structure by changing the plane of polarization yet without upsetting the balance of the body, then mutation occurs (one sees new insights into the theory of mutations and possibly a support for reincarnation).

What role does color play in mutation, cancer, and tumors?

In tumors and cancer, where there is strain, color can reverse the process and return the cell to normal by removing the strainer because it is in the pattern or nature of the cell to return to normal structure. Another way to say it would be that the cell has the tendency to return to its normal structure if it can. In mutations, where there is no strain, color protects the new organism so that it can function in its environment by giving it all the conditions necessary for survival because life is color.

This action can be phrased in a capsule:

If altered function takes place **with strain,** then tumors result.

If altered function takes place **without strain,** then mutations result.

Theory of Color — the Cosmic Spiral as a Bridge of Healing

The author has theorized about how color heals in cancer and tumors, how color protects the mutants, and how color plays the vital role in keeping man in harmony. Now he seeks to explain how color evolves as a spiral — a principle basic to nature's laws.

The spiral can be seen everywhere. Tendrils wind around a support; flowers form in a spiral nature; leaves are coiled in spiral form before they open; a tendril shoots literally by spiral growth to screw its way through a hard surface. The spiral of shells is well-known, and mention is made of the conch shell in the **Upanishads** as well as the spiral movement in the Chinese interpretation of the Yin and Yang forces for the **I Ching** Hexagram.

The spiral is discerned in many organs of the body, and a spiral movement is seen in many of its functions. It seems most significant that all creatures, from the lowly amoeba to man, when moving without any means of stimulation being involved, are urged in a spiral path. Horns are spiral; the umbilical cord is spiral; the sweat glands, the humerus, the pelvis, and the thumb prints are spiral; in cell division, the spiral appears and even in mathematics, a logarithmic spiral occurs.[14]

Linus Pauling, Nobel Prize winner, discovered what may be said to be Polarized Molecules. The strings which form the structure have a spiral motif with the joining units linked together to form a helix in the shape of a loosely coiled spring: like a symmetrical spiral staircase with each step made of a different kind of wood. These molecular units of matter are quite unsymmetrical, like a glove or a shoe which can have two forms that are mirror images of each other. **All the spirals of living matter twine the same way around . . .** although things would work equally well the other way around.

As Sir Laurence Bragg, another Nobel Prize winner, states, "We are built of right-handed corkscrews."

In his book **The Secret of Life,** Lakhovsky drew an analogy between the spiral formation to be found in living cells and the coin in an electrical current. He suggested that just as in an electrical oscillating circuit, radiations are emitted through the functioning of a spiral of wire increasing its capacity, so in the living cell radiations are emitted in a like manner.

14. See H.W. Heason, **Frontiers of Understanding,** Ritter Press (n.d.) Nottingham, England.

The spiral seems to have some subtle quality of its own. When a piece of copper is wound into a spiral, it acquires properties it did not previously possess. Used mechanically, the spiral is a means by which it is possible to penetrate wood or iron. In electronics, the spiral is used to convert radio waves into electrical impulses. In the widest sense, it suggests nothing so much as the capacity to move from one level to another or from one vibration to another.

How does this spiral theory apply to the cosmos? Wilhelm Reich has an interesting observation in his **Cosmic-Super-Imposition.** Briefly, he stated that the moon and the earth flow along Orgone streams in the form of spirals. The moon thereby falls toward a point in space where the center of the earth either has been or will be, but not where it is. This gives a mutual spiral intertwining movement for both which, to the observer on earth, suggests that the moon revolves around the earth (this is also partially the theory of relativity).

In his work with Orgone, the life force that he believed permeated the universe, Reich observed that life began on earth from its action. From his study of the tiny sparks of light which appeared in an over-charged chamber, it became clear that the movement of these took the form of a spiral with alternate large and small loops. Following up the idea that the fusion of two of these streams was creative, as in the sex act, he likened the creation of heavenly bodies to the creation of a new life in the womb. In the heavens vast streams of Orgone energy flow, pulsating in spiral form, creating through super-imposition.

To Reich, light is an Orgonetic effect with a characteristic bluish color, like oxygen, which is illuminated when excited with electricity. Since he regarded it as the vital force needed to sustain life, Reich used Orgone, a form of light, in vibration therapy for healing cancer and emotional illness. To him, the origin of energy is the sun and the Orgone ocean is in a constant state of flux; thus light is composed of excitation and lumination. Light, he said, does not travel through space; only excitation travels through space; and when it reaches an area where local conditions make it possible, an Orgone lumination occurs, and this visible phenomenon is called light. Orgone flows from a weaker to a stronger system. Life would cease if the flow ran on as in the physical state which is from the stronger to the weaker. The Orgone — a blue light — would restore balance and harmony (Reich's **Orgone Box** has been banned in the United States, but it is used in other parts of the world. Further, one school of psychology uses Reich's technique in the treatment of the emotionally disturbed patient).

Interesting parallels may be drawn with Reich's theory. Bechamp, the magnificent intellectual giant, observed, and many other bacteriologists agree with him, that Microzymates, which he discovered in his research work, are the fundamental basis of life, and these Microzymates can never be destroyed. On death, they leave the body and return to the atmosphere. The Hindus consider prahna to be the vital force of life, and it too is never destroyed. Are Reich, Bechamp, and the Hindus saying the same thing, but with different descriptive terminologies and from different points of view? Bechamp sees the source of life from a microscopic view (Microzymates); Reich, from a macroscopic view (Orgone); the Hindus, from a combined microscopic and macroscopic view. It is not within the scope of this book to pursue this matter (for further information, see the author's **Nu Reflex Therapy**).

The philosopher Bergson had another theory, for it was his opinion that acquired structural and functional modifications may be hereditarily transmitted under certain conditions, one of which is desire. Bergson stated the eye was produced because the organism had the desire to see, and he added that if function builds up structure, then "matter is hindbound with habit."

If recurring types of stimuli build up in time permanent substates of response, an organism is simply "bound energy." This theory is important because man sees color and also feels color.

Both the eye and the skin are used in color therapy. But another clue may be found in Radionics, especially with reference to the De La Warr Camera and his experimentation with this radionic instrument. De La Warr came to the conclusion that the machine does not diagnose physical effects, but made contact with some underlying Primitive or Basic energy beneath the physical in which patterns exist and from which physical symptoms arise. He noticed that there were cases where no obvious illness existed, yet where some potentiality to a particular ailment was involved. It seemed that the root cause of illness lay deep in some subatomic[15] field on which the activities of the mind play an important part. Emotional effects thus became causes and had to be added to his diagnostic list. The underlying pattern of energy is obviously very complex, but it has been found that the whole complexity attached to the personality is contained in a very small portion of the anatomy. So that by the use of a simple spot of blood, saliva or hair, the characteristics of a whole person could be analyzed.[16] It is possible to take a spot of blood, says De La Warr, and by means of the diagnostic instrument, discover not only what disease the patient is suffering from, but its cause, which may be very complex. Because potentiality to disease and not the disease itself is being determined, the techniques of radionics in healing or the methods devised by radionics are eschewed at the present time by the medical profession as unorthodox (unscientific?).

Radionics obliterates space when space signifies a measure of distance. But space is not empty. It is filled with color, sound, vibration. Radionics annihilates space-distance, but in reality, it uses the life-giving forces in space for healing; therefore radionics is the new space medicine today. Color thus becomes an ancillary to radionic space-medicine, for it reaches from earth, being rooted in the soil as plants, out into the cosmos, and from the cosmos back into the earth. Here the principle of the spiral bridge could also be applied to color: color connects earth, plant-life, animals, and man to the universe; color evolves like a spiral or like a corkscrew and color effects changes on all levels by way of its vibrations, which shift as they go from one level to another.

15. See F.S. Northrop and H.S. Burr.

16. Dr. B. Bhattacharyya, in **The Science of Cosmic Ray Therapy,** believes that this type of analysis can be done with the photograph of a patient, and he goes even further to state that changes in the human organs are reflected in the photograph (Baroda 1957).

These experiments in radionics deal with effects far more fundamental than the physical since all matter is ultimately vibration. The obvious conclusion to be reached is that well-being is the result of harmony within the complex system of vibration involved in the organic structure of the body. This seeming radionic "detour" from the matter of light as directly applied to color and healing has been dictated by the nature of man's search to understand the many ramifications of light, color, and life.

Mention should here be made of how Yale University developed a highly sensitive instrument capable of measuring electrical discharges in the body as small as five millionth of a volt. Their research workers Burr and Northrop succeeded in establishing conclusive evidence—after probing with this delicate device the subtle electrical variations which accompany all processes of growth — that the electrical potential found in the human body is directly related to an electrical pattern. Rife's findings about the color of the micro-organism and the way in which a change in nutrient changes the color because it changes the organism are so profound that his work with the extraordinary technique that he devised is discussed in another section of this book dealing with the "Healing Powers of the Individual Colors."

What is the relation of electrical energies to color and sound? This relationship will be clarified — as analysis continues — but a generalisation is in order about the forms: **light, sound, heat, magnetism, color and electrical energies are all different forms of one source of energy,** and they differ only in frequency of vibration and medium of conduction. Once the **interchangeability of these six forms** is understood, a different approach to healing the total man by means of color can be more readily cultivated.

Maryla De Chrapowicki, in **Biotonic Therapy,** states

... the law of life is motion, a rhythmic cyclic pulsation of radiant energy which always tends to preserve and restore balance and harmony... its measured periodic vibrations throbbing through space complete with every beat, a minor cycle within the major wave of the

33

great cycle of evolution. As this rhythmic factor becomes more and more evident, so does man begin to notice the unfoldment of an intricate pattern of radioactive substances which act as a bridge between the tangible and the intangible or tenuous states of life, and this bridge reveals a synthetic unity of mind and body. Life is a manifestation of a ceaseless exchange between various degrees of matter. The character of the energy implanted in the body during that activity is, above all, **ionic** before it becomes **molecular,** for it proceeds from the sphere of radiation. But man perceives only the secondary physical effects, those which manifest on the plane of matter and which are recognized as **molecular** activity.

This purely physical approach is the basis of biochemistry. The emphasis is on molecular activity as though it were the only reality, for the biochemist either forgets or is unaware that molecular activity relates only to a final process and not to the fundamental curative impulses which stimulate these molecules to activity. The Burr and Northrop studies established conclusively that the electrical potential found in the human body is directly related to an electrical pattern; this pattern dictates the nature of the organism, but it is not an inflexible form; rather it is a patterning principle in the sense that it evolves and changes. As the patterning evolves, so the organism evolves, assumes form, grows, matures, remains constant; then the organism builds new cells but always organizes them after the original design. The organism is recreated, but always with the pattern dictated. The patterning here is a dynamic process, not a static entity. There is almost a suggestion of simultaneity as a principle, but it does not work out as simultaneity of pattern and form. This reservation applies: the patterning has an implicit form that it communicates to the organism. Is this the principle of determinism? The cabbage in the sub-atomic field results in a cabbage. It cannot become a rose. The patterning is determined in the sub-atomic field and given the same environment, it evolves with fidelity; electrical vibration here is a force that can be likened to the force required to construct hundreds of Empire State buildings. This force works to incarnate the patterning in the emerging cellular entity: to form the lion, the rose, the man, the diamond, the drop of oil, illness, health. It is the pulsating rhythm of form and pattern that is termed life. It is potential, patterning, and form that reflect the three principles of structural integrity, organism-rejuvenation, and regeneration. The Hindus have conveniently summed these ideas in their Triad of Creator, Preserver, and Destroyer: Brahma, Vishnu and Siva.

Do these electrical impulses put into effect what the author has called the Law of Evolutionary Redundancy? Before that question can be answered and before these various ideas can be summarized with respect to color healing, a final word is necessary about the emotions and the electro-magnetic principles relating to electrical potential.

Basically, emotion is an expressive plasmic response. Pleasurable stimuli, the right vibrations cause an emotion of the protoplasm from the centre to the periphery. Conversely, unpleasurable stimuli, the wrong vibrations, cause an emotion from the periphery to the centre of the organism. These two basic directions of bio-physical plasmic currents correspond to the two basic effects of the emotional apparatus: pleasure and pain. The physical plasmic motion and the corresponding emotional sensations are functionally identical. They are indivisible. It is known that they are functionally not only identical but also antithetical at the same time; bio-physical plasmic excitation results in a sensation, and a sensation is expressed in plasmic motion. This emotion is related to the basic life force itself. Pleasurable emotion is moving out, expanding, being field-oriented growth; unpleasurable emotion is being withdrawn, ego-centric, and inhibited.

The decline of the electrical potential begins usually during the latter part of life, and any deviation from the normal that may occur before the allotted time of natural decline indicates that fundamental changes detrimental to health and dangerous to life are taking place in the body. There is an electro-magnetic principle of formative energy guiding the integration of matter and controlling the structural differentiation of all organisms. Only upon such a principle are these three aspects of life made possible:

1. individual distinction of structural integrity
2. organic rejuvenation, and
3. regeneration.

Because of this principle, this interaction is not only possible, but also imperative. Therefore the chief aim of all healing methods should be directed towards the preservation, restoration, and regeneration of electrical potential for it is in the electrical potential of an organism that the key is found to the solution of the miracle of cure. Here is the **Open Sesame** to cure; **the subatomic area.** The cabbage can become a rose; mutations can occur when the environment changes; evolution and revolution take place with colour vibration.

How is cure possible? It may be said by means of atomic action. The introduction into the body of electromagnetic remedies is not followed by a physical assimilation, but by an atomic explosion which releases energy imprisoned by muscular rigidity, anxiety, and incorrect breathing. Thereby the normal molecular motion is re-established.

Dinsah Ghadiali, one of the foremost pioneers in color therapy, points out that:

1. Light itself is imponderable yet is able to produce chemical reaction in plants. Light has an electrochemical effect upon the retina of the eye and indirectly upon the optic nerve which makes vision possible.
2. Atropine even when diluted more than a million fold produces dilation of the pupils of man and animals.
3. The inorganic substances which serve plants for nutrition are taken up by them only in infinitesimal quantities.
4. Hydrochloric acid when diluted a thousand times with water easily dissolves fibrin and gluten at body temperature but this solvent power is lessened if the proportion of acid in the solution is increased
5. The mineral water found to have its greatest curative effect contains minerals in very minute amounts.

The Hindus approach this problem from another viewpoint. In the work of Ayurveda is found an attempt to explain a relationship between the elements in nature and the principles of the human body. There the three Doshas refer to the five elements.[17] Akasa, or ether, Air, Fire, Water, and Earth. These three Doshas are distributed among the five great elements constituting the cosmos.

1. The first Dosha Vayu or harmony is composed of Akasa and Air.
2. The second Dosha Pitta or energy is composed of fire.
3. The third Dosha Kapha or inertia is composed of water and earth.

Harmony, energy, and inertia are a three-fold force which contains primordial matter and is inherent in every living cell. According to Dr. Bhattacharyya's analysis of the three Gunas, which are the cosmic attributes of the three Doshas, Sattva is neutral, Rajas is negative, and Tamas is positive. Other Hindus differ with this view, and so does the author. The author further adds that despite the differences in the interpretations of the Gunas, there is agreement about the explanation of them.

The three attributes are in constant motion—uniting, separating, and uniting again, giving shape and form to all things. Bhattacharyya says that whatever energy there is in the phenomenal world is the result of Rajas alone. All matter of resistance and stability is due to Tamas, and all conscious manifestation is due to Sattva. The three Doshas correspond to the three Gunas or cosmic attributes. Thus Vayu is conscious manifestation, Pitta is energy, and Kapha is resistance or inertia. Whenever Pitta (energy) is retarded in its action, it is due to Kapha (inertia). When Pitta decreases, Kapha increases and the reverse is also true; in both cases, Vayu, the principle of harmony and equilibrium, is disturbed. As man grows older, Kapha increases while Pitta decreases, and the harmony of the three at-

---

17. The Indian version of the five elements is different from the Chinese. Both agree on earth, fire and water. The Chinese stress metal and wood as the other two elements, unlike the Indian. To account for this difference is very enlightening; but such a discussion does not fall in the purview of this study.

tributes is disturbed (entropy). This accounts for aging. Color therapy can and does restore this equilibrium if applied properly.

TABLE 1.

Relations of Gunas to Elements: According to Bhattacharyya[18]

GUNAS	FORCES	DOSHAS	ELEMENTS
Sattva	Harmony	Vayu	Akasa and Air
Rajas	Energy	Pitta	Fire
Tamas	Inertia	Kapha	Water and Earth

TABLE 2.

Author's Changes of the Bhattacharyya Table

Gunas or Cosmic Attributes	Qualities	Forces or Principles of Three Doshas	Doshas	Color	Elements	Polarity
Sattva	Life, Light, Freshness, Resolution, Good Moral-Quality, Proton	Harmony or Equilibrium	Vayu	B. Blue V. Violet	Akasa or Ether and Air	Positive
Rajas	Activity, Electron	Energy	Pitta	R. Red Y. Yellow	Fire	Negative
Tamas	Sleep Dullness, Decay Neutron	Inertia or Resistance	Kapha	O. Orange I. Indigo G. Green	Water and Earth	Neutral

18. D. Bhattacharyya, *op. cit.*, p. 37.

Certain mystics and alchemists disagree with the color-chart in Number 1 Table and claim that the colors are as follows:

The Colors of the Elements and Their "Complementaries"

ELEMENT	COLOR	COMPLEMENTARY COLOR
Ether	Indigo	Dark Amber
Air	Blue	Orange
Fire	Red	Green
Water	White (Silver)	Black (Grey)
Earth	Yellow	Violet

Some day, perhaps, the physicist, the physiologist, and the psychologist will be able to find their way through these mazes of imperfect interpretation and not behave like the blind men identifying the elephant (a fable that needs no repetition) or like the inmate in the mental institution who, as the story goes, was writing himself a letter. When the patient was asked by the psychiatrist what he was doing, he calmly replied, "Writing a letter." The psychiatrist was pleased and asked the patient, "To whom are you writing?" Again the patient calmly replied, "To myself, of course!" The doctor then inquired, "What are you writing about?" To that, the patient replied, "I don't know; I haven't received the letter yet."

This dilemma is termed a **Double Bind** in Zen Buddhism. No matter what question the doctor asks, he gets into deeper difficulties and he traps himself; so it is when one reviews the different interpretations of color that are dictated by the mind-set of various individuals.

1. To the realist, the color red of the rose is in the rose.
2. To the physicist, the color of the rose depends on the reflected light.
3. To the physiologist, the hue of the rose *is* red when looked at directly, but it is yellow or grey as an attribute of the eye.

4. To the psychologist, the red of the rose is neither the attribute of the flower, nor the characteristic of light, nor a manifestation in the eyes; instead it is purely subjective and it is in the eyes of the beholder.
5. To the painter, the rose is his creation on the canvas.
6. To the writer like Gertrude Stein, a rose is a rose is a rose remains a semantic reflection of the patterned responses of people.

What may one conclude from the realization of how mind-set determines end-view? What relationship is there among the Gunas, the Doshas, color as vibration of light, aging, and death? Does man have to age? For the moment, let theories and different generalizations bespeak their own inter-relationship and dictate the identity of ideas.

1. Light is more than the visible spectrum.
2. Light has dynamic qualities still unknown to us; it is an unknown phenomenon that demands further study.
3. Thought is vibration, a most powerful vibration that **can annihilate space and time.**
4. **Thought is color.**
5. Right thinking keeps the body in balance; wrong thinking leads to emotional distress and disharmony.
6. Immortality: The physiologists say the cell can regenerate itself endlessly if there is no pathology, no strain. Theoretically, then, life can be eternal, barring accidents.
7. Eastern thought shows that man and the universe are composed of the same elements; one affects the other, and they are inter-related. The healing must come from within and go outward; from above, downward. The West attacks disease from without. Germs are treated with drugs; but the germ is one of many strainers. Are germs the cause or the result of disease? In the answer to this question is the reason for allopathic medicine's failure to project a tenable philosophy.
8. The psychologists opened up for the West an awareness of the reaches of the mind into the unconscious and the sub-

conscious, ideas old to the East. Freud showed how the unconscious affected the physical body; Jung began to intrude a metaphysical slant that contrasted with the conditioned reflex as a mechanistic theory.

9. Coue and Mesmer opened up the area of suggestion. Auto-hypnosis and hypno-analysis have evolved.

10. Psychosomatic medicine is coming into its own by stressing that the psyche affects the soma (both psyche and somatic strainers cause altered function or pathology).

11. The Indian practitioner today — if the Eastern healer has not been corrupted by Western allopathic medical practices — relates the Doshas to the three forces of the universe as Harmony, Energy, and Inertia, and out of these all life evolves. They have their color equivalents which spell the words **Roygbiv or Vibgyor** in reverse. Harmony, life and color are intertwined.

12. The chiropractors say that if one keeps pressure off the spinal column, he will not age.

13. F. M. Alexander observed that if the Primary Control is not disturbed, then one will not age or be ill. Here age is not to be confused with maturation.

14. The analysis of the physics of light provides both static and dynamic interpretations: The Quantum and the Wave theories of light and perception have not been inter-related to the health of man, his illnesses, and his relation through color/vibration to the universe. The dynamists have proved that light and color are active field forces. Steiner, as educator and healer, has philosophized about man's relation to color and vibration. Simpson, Lehr, and Flammarion may or may not have theorized about the function and role of color, but the experiments must be related to those generalizations for which some of the scientists have been crucified and others, en "NOBEL"ed: Reich and his Orgone theory, work in radionics, the De La Warr machine, the Burr-Northrop contribution, the theory of the spiral, biotonics, color in the nitrogen cycle and in the drop of water. All these emerging fragments give man his position as a color-thought-vibration,

an upthrust of color, both within and without the body. Man is a vibration on the forty-ninth level, and he must be so treated. Every vibration within himself affects him and he, in turn, is affected by these pounding vibrations surrounding him and in which he lives and breathes.

The theories mentioned have validity and cogency, but no interpretation explains all aspects bearing upon the phenomenon of color. Rudolf Steiner comes perhaps the closest to an understanding of the inter-relationship of color to life. These views have, however, one factor in common: Though some may range from the macroscopic view of light and others to the microscopic, no one submits a theory that explains the total phenomena of color and light vibrations as they affect man, animal and plant and certainly not specifically with regard to color as a healing power man can use.

The author has sought to present the different interpretations in an effort to show how compartmentalization has been the hallmark of their sterling representations of color. Each theory has a genuineness and an effectiveness that cannot be disputed; but the various authorities taking only one part of the vibration/color have not stressed that all life is vibration in form and number and that the whole scale of life is color, as the author does. The various observers have explained only one aspect of color, a part of the scale, and one or more vibration frequencies; no one has applied this theory to the total scale or its adaptability to the various levels that explain life and its multifarious vibrations. They are playing "Chopsticks" on the color-sound board. The concerto is now being written.

Because color contains this entire scale, with its seven visible rays as well as with its other invisible rays, because life is color itself, color has healing power, so affirms the author.

Because life is color, color prolongs life, cures imbalance in life or destroys life. The seven visible colors and the other invisible colors must vibrate to keep harmonious balance and rhythmic functioning, affirms the author. Any disturbance of rhythmic harmony creates imbalance and too great an imbalance causes death. But in harmony is found eternal life. Death is banished.

The author—speculating on all these different views, these slanted observations conditioned by one's education, environment, and social "time-binding" factors regardless of the time or the culture—says that man can live eternally. There need be no aging and no awareness of time. If there is no change in body balance and if color is correctly used, man can have his Shangri-La now without the fuss and bother of passports, changing money, or learning a foreign language. "If," as Kipling says, is a little word with enormous possibilities.

If one thinks right, projects his color awareness to keep his body in balance, he can live forever. This is the secret of life, provided he is not hit by a space missile.

Allopathic medicine with its reliance upon the germ theory fails to provide the answer to man's illness. Its wrong theory and wrong application have mired the physicians in the slough of slaughter. Some regard man as a liver or a lung, but not as an integrated whole; others make him a machine subject to stimulus-response. The few who combine the psychosomatic approach tend to neglect the relationship to man's internal and external environment. Still others place man in a vacuum, in a laboratory, or else study the dead body (morbid anatomy) to treat the living. Medicine is standing on its head and does not know it. The time has come for it to stand on its own feet with a set of sound philosophic values and techniques.

The psychologists are shifting roles; many are trying to become psychiatrists whereas the psychiatrists seek to become psychologists. But at least they are toying with the inner and the outer man. They seek to release the patient's anxiety and tension, but do not tell the suffering individual how to succeed. But one paean of praise, one hallelujah for their broadcast that the emotions of man are more important than the germs in his body.

The sociologists try to explain man as a product of his outer environment, but forget or neglect to note that the inner environment is, in many cases, more important than the outer. They have signalized that environmental factors are just as important as hereditary factors. The historians, seeking to explain traditions, have made a sacred cow out of the past: impersonalizing man in their reports of wars and epochs and losing sight of man's psychological and physiological needs. Man cannot be impersonalized, but the historian continues to impersonalize man and to personalize events.

The occultists are concerned mainly with the spiritual aspects and tend to forget that man has a body, a fact of considerable importance. But at least they have been forerunners of those changes made in healing that are beginning to appear on the Western horizon. Their approach is more scientific — in the popular sense of the word — than is the approach of the present-day scientists. Perhaps therein is the explanation for the oddity of scientists today seeking to become occultists.

The New Thought movement has been accompanied by a different training of the clergy, whether priest, rabbi, or minister. The various schools of pastoral care and the many foundations with their grants stress the need of training the minister not only in theology, but also in psychology, psychiatry, and sociology so that parishioners' needs may be met. Is the minister returning to the role of the doctor-priest that history has recounted? At least the ministry is aware in its educational program as well as in its practices that man functions on many levels and it is moving in that direction with glacier-like solidity and momentum.

But certain theoreticians have begun to abandon the medieval fortress of allopathic medicine. Singled out here is Selye, who demonstrated that man responds to stress (G-A-S), which can be any one of a multitude of stimuli. What man calls disease is nothing more than the **natural** response of the body to stress and strain. Selye's views are to be coupled with the slanted generalizations made by Freud, Jung, F. M. Alexander, Bergson, Coue and the pioneers in New Thought movement. They all can be likened to riders on a train coming into New York from Miami. The other train headed for New York is coming from the opposite direction: Montreal, Canada. This express is carrying the theoreticians — orthodox and unorthodox — who have wrestled with the problem of color and vibration and their effects on man. Some are unusual for their imaginative grasp of the total picture (Steiner), but others moored to their particular experiments, have no desire to leap out

44

into the theoretical explorations that their findings naturally dictate.

When both trains meet at the central railroad terminal, the passengers melt into one crowd that merges into a total sea of pulsating ideas that ebb and flow. These theoreticians, whatever their view, have readied the Western mind for an appreciation of the role that color and vibration must play in the life of man and of the cosmos. Now the directional flow is to apply these insights to man's body and the cure of his illness. The dynamists in reinterpreting the forces of the universe have devised a theory of the spiral and described an orgone blue to indicate that the force in nature is similarly a force in man and further that this force is characterized by color which is as basic to healing as it is to the movement of the constellations or the nebulae in the skies. Color, forgotten as an element in the water molecule and in the nitrogen cycle, together with vibration is used in radionics and biotonics as a vital part of life and as a key to healing, whether or not man is conscious of these forces.

The Indians with their account of the three Doshas have provided an account of how the forces within also work without. Man today must begin to harmonize himself with the color / vibrations surrounding him for he affects the surround and the surround affects him by way of the color-vibration on the spectrum or beyond the spectrum. He has accepted the miracle of X-rays, but he has not gone beyond the X-rays to realize how his food intake is nothing but the breakdown of color; to realize that his diseases must be treated not by drugs in response to the germ theory, but by changing his vibrations. Here is the answer to the new world of space upon which many has already entered.

Man must change in his utilization consciously of the color sea in which he is immersed and from which he draws his life sustenance. Otherwise he will be drowned in the vibrations of illness; he will be drowned in the vibrations of the past, which is the term used here for traditions that can destroy if they are not changed and reinterpreted or readjusted to man's awareness of himself in the presence of the moment; he will be drowned in the vibrations of his ignorance about himself wherein he misuses his wave lengths. Socrates very sagely remarked, "Know Thyself," and Western thought has followed the Greeks in allowing man to know himself as a political animal. But today, the Socratic dictum must be rephrased; **Know yourself as your color dictates.** No reference is here intended to the red of Russia, the color lines of the early Indian cast system, the demarcations of segregation or the Apartheid. Color is the same for all. In knowing himself as color, man knows all humanity. In healing himself by color, he heals the ills of mankind.

CHAPTER 2

COLOR AND LIGHT: VIEWS OF THE PAST

In this section, the historical approach appraising the theories of color healing advocated by other cultures will consider the contributions made by Egypt, Iran, India, and China as well as the lore taught by mythology, astrology, and the occultists. All of these generalizations reveal a vast knowledge of light and color, but some of them are lost in the pages of the past. These findings the modern scientists are beginning to rediscover piece-meal and to utilize, but, in most instances, without any philosophic bases and, what is more strange, without too much insight into the significance of their findings with regard to healing. The past does provide a key, especially in mythology, but in most countries the past lies buried in a mass of dogma, ritual, and tradition; the spade work done by scientists does not always present the total picture.

How is mythology the macroscopic view of man as he follows the race experience and instinct for self-preservation where his senses are not corrupted by civilization and where he must worship a hero? The hero helps man reduce the strain within. This is the innate patterning potential to get back on the road so man can survive. How is the cell the microscopic view of man as he follows his instinct for self-preservation? When the cell adjusts to a strainer by reverting to its earlier evolutionary pathways, it is using the wisdom of the body which lies imbedded in its sub-atomic structural patterning potential. Cell and myth both follow the same patterning.

Religion is related to mythology and when man creates god in his own image, he is ascribing superhuman characteristics to this god. Why? Among other reasons, to reduce his anxiety and tension. Color does this as the myths reveal. The colors of the gods are red, white, blue, green, like the colors of the flag, not gray. The organism must revert to its original pattern to survive. The cell and the myth serve as a unit, one within and the other without. The cell has embedded in itself a feedback process to utilize the myth for the preservation of the race because the myth is the fundamental basis for the release of abnormal tension and restoration of harmony. The myth is the true sensor-antenna of the environment, and it gives man the right information, puts him on the right frequency. When he loses the pathway, the myth is his compass that directs him back to health.

Was Krishna a man or a god? The heroes in mythology are created by the people to answer their particular ideology or needs. Why do they assess the gods as color equivalents or as electromagnetic field forces? How are they able to describe positive and negative currents and the metabolic processes of the person, the race, and the universe? Mythology herein furnishes an evolutionary proof of the unconscious wisdom of the people, the instinct of the self-preservation of humanity that is curiously coupled with the instinct of hero-worship: e.g., the mythologizing aspects of ennobling Gandhi, Lincoln, Kennedy or Lenin. The poet has been termed the unheralded legislator of the future because he voices the eternal truths that transcend the personal needs of man and the historical role of tradition. Mythology is the unheralded projection of the wisdom of the human instincts told in "color"ful tales about heroes who once lived, but who became ennobled, sanctified "haloized"; tales that reveal the directional drift and response of man to the submerged icebergs of his unconscious response to archetypal patterns associated with color. Mythology reflects how the wisdom of the race heals itself by devices of which it may or may not be conscious.

Another interpretation of the myth must be briefly mentioned: the occult and hidden meanings. Is the myth about the hero turned God an attempt by the In-group to teach the initiates its secrets and to confuse the Out-group? Or does mythology go beyond: to show the wisdom of the race in healing itself by devices of which it is completely unconscious?

The East is becoming Westernized and the West is immersing itself in Eastern philosophy, but reinterpreting it from its own slanted needs. East and West, however, do not meet in their interpretation of mythology. With Jung, mysticism and mythology were scientifically reappraised to furnish another key for unlocking the secret of man. Psychology, sociology and history took new directions. Mythology poses a problem related to man's quest of the self. Where does the man-hero end and where does the god-function take over? What makes people create gods of their heroes? The matter posed by Krishna in Indian mythology serves West as well as East with an example that reflects certain basic truths but here East differs from the West in interpretation.

Of all the countries to be considered, perhaps China and India are most significant for their contributions to man's use of color in healing and for man's awareness of self. Not only did they make an impact on their own culture but also did they influence others beyond the confines of their territories. How they affected each other cannot be said since they both exchanged ideas with such ease as well as rapidity that one cannot readily unweave the closely woven tapestry of their ideas. Basic to this consideration is the far-reaching influence of Chinese and Indian teachings on the world of the past.

At this point, reference is made to the reports of the 1962 XXXV World Congress of Anthropologists held in Mexico. Over twelve hundred scholars from all over the world participated, and the highlight of the reports was the provocative argument between the Diffusionists and the Independent Inventionists about the effects of Buddhist and Hindu India, Japan, and China on the people of Meso-America. Though the matter was not ultimately settled about the outside influences on American origins, there was no denying the stir of interest raised by the observation that the Aztec Calendar was really a Chinese invention, that a Chinese monk had landed in Mexico 412 A. D., and that the Japanese of Asia had settled on the coast of Alaska. But other eminent archaeologists affirmed that the Chinese who had traveled to the coast of Mexico and Latin America had observed the then splendid culture and had returned to China enriched with many ideas and modes of the Latin American Indian culture.[1]

1. The author here wishes to add that during the course of his travels, he noted in the Museum at Anuradhapura on the island of Ceylon—the various items bearing witness to contacts 2,500 years ago with Greece, Rome, and the early Chinese travelers.

The positions taken by the Diffusionists and the Inventionists are illuminating since they show aspects of the problem with which this book is concerned: namely, the reaches of the influence of the mind and consciousness of self and body. Did the Chinese give the Indians the idea for the Mayan Aztec Calendar? Or did the American Indian give the Chinese the ideas? What other idea percolated through the minds of the people who came and then departed for their home lands? The answers to these questions rest with the scholars and the anthropologists... be they Diffusionist or Inventionist. The author is in no position to attempt answers to these knotty matters. What is to be stressed is that no matter which road was taken for the advance of civilization, the end goal was the acquisition of a body of information about healing and the awareness of the self in its relation to the laws of the universe. Whether the **materia medica**[2] came from India or China or was indigenous to the particular culture in which it had its birth is not for him to determine; he is concerned here with the material of their awareness.

The Sacred Mushroom, Ladder of Mystical Experience, Alcoholism and Drug Addiction

The ancient and some modern primitive tribes — like the Mixes, Zapotecs, and the Chatinos of Mexico — and the tribes of Northeastern Siberia — the Chuckchees, Korjaks, and the Tungus — believe that their intuitive capacity is increased by eating certain species of mushrooms and in this way they can cure their disease. Anthropological evidence shows that civilizations are divided into two groups: the mushroom eaters and the non-mushroom eaters who believed that the fleshy fungus was poisonous and therefore tabu. (Was this a device for the in-group to keep the secret of the mushroom to themselves?)

2. Royle says that Hippocrates, the father of Western medicine, borrowed his **Materia Medica** from India. Garrison reports that Aristotle is believed to be indebted to Hindu physicians and surgeons.

The mushroom Armanita Muscaria was and is being used by the mystics of India to this day. My Indian friends (in 1964) told me that the ritual of Soma — which never has been positively identified — mentioned in the **Rig-Veda** certainly matches very closely the traditional picture of ecstasy described in literature. All who have participated in the eating of the "Sacred" mushroom report a heightening of the senses and an awareness of brilliant color, such as is not at present seen on this earth (to be compared with Huxley's account of his response to mescalin in his experiments). As in the dream state, they seem to see or relive the myths of the past: what Jung calls the **Collective Unconscious** and Fromm, the **Forgotten Language**. On the physical plane, this phenomenon may explain what Cannon calls the **Wisdom of the Body**. How does the mushroom trigger off the latent color in the body to increase the extra-sensory perception mechanism of the individual? This electrical field-force **zeros-in** to the latent patterning embedded in the sub-atomic field-force of the cell on which is recorded — for all time and for any one who wishes to tune in on it the race wisdom made manifest in mythology and in dreams. The mushroom is one of many devices by which this feed-back process is stimulated. Both the mushroom and meditation stimulate a color vibration which opens up the channel of cosmic communication.

Trial and error have been eliminated in the sub-atomic field. If the organism in the past received too much wrong information dangerous to its development, it either died or else devised a method—motion and remotion, attraction and repulsion — to cope with its environment. The organism that withstood the strain imprinted this knowledge on the tape of the sub-atomic, material that could be described first as the wisdom of the body and then as the wisdom of the race. When the person presses the right button — the right color vibration — the record is automatically played back, similar to the playback from the juke box when the coin is dropped into the slot. The evolutionary process here has recorded its experience on the electrical tape of the sub-atomic field force which always responds to the right vibration.

The oracles of ancient Greece were familiar with the use of inhaling carbon dioxide or other gases to heighten the senses.

Mention is here made of how the Terpenes — camphor and frankincense — are used in the ritual of China, Tibet, and India to induce the same effect. A jump in time may be made from the Greek to the Celt. Much in folk-lore and mythology reveals that the mushroom is found in the vicinity of the oak tree. The Celts who used herbs in healing and who associated herbology with their folk-lore, ranked the mistletoe which grew on and near the oak trees as a gift from the gods.

Did Hercules derive his strength by eating of the mushroom? In some way, man is able to slip on to another wave length or vibration. Were the sooth-sayers empowered mysteriously to become mystics because they ate the mushrooms, inhaled carbon dioxide or one of the terpenes to change their wave length? Did Buddha eat of the mushroom or Christ or Moses? Is the charismatic leader who has removed himself from society and who returns, mysteriously enlightened, a "mushroom eater"? Is manna, feeding a people in the wilderness, not interpreted by some authorities as a form of food responsible for the mystical visions in the Bible as individualized by the experience of certain Sensitives? Is the mysticism of the Old Testament a tapping into the sea of Cosmic Intelligence?

The scientific study of the mystic experience must always include reference to William James. But first among the modern scientists who reported this change of preception, this sweep or insight by way of inhaling carbon dioxide was Sir Humphrey Davy in April of 1794. William James after reading his account and **The Anaesthetic Revelation and the Gist of Philosophy** (Amsterdam N.Y., 1874) sought to study the phenomenon. The result is his classic on **The Varieties of the Religious Experience.** Huxley, Wasson, and many others have advanced this type of experimentation so that the West is now coming to grips with certain aspects of thought vibration and extrasensory perception. Here publication of their findings broadcasts those generalizations that were, in the past, known only to the select few, the elite in the culture, like the priest-doctor who transmitted his secrets orally. But these important developments in research are slanted to discover psychological causes of disease, not the total relation of the color vibration to the total man.

One may pursue this matter to discuss the methodical cultivation of the mystical experience pursued among the Yogis, the Sufis, the Christians and contrast their findings with those to whom the mystic experience was a sporadic occurrence, but the purpose of this book must not be deflected. Instead, one must seek to determine what happens to the individual who has opened up certain channels for better or worse. For some the mushroom has been a significant experience. Certainly a change in the vibrations of the body takes place. For others, alcohol, drugs, nitrous oxide, ether, "LSD", and mescalin have affected the vibrations. Consciously or unconsciously, man must experience this vibration or color glow which is the doorway to healing. Is color the open sesame to mounting the ladder of intuitive insight and revelation? Is the alcoholic an addict because the habit is the result of his tuning-in on certain vibrations or has his tuning in on these vibrations led to the habit? The ladder of mystic experience has many rungs on which one climbs toward that insight leading to samadhi or cosmic consciousness, and the rung labeled "Alcohol, Nitrous Oxide or Ether" is one of the lowest in position on the upward climb. Is the alcoholic in his heightened awareness misusing the vibration by using the wrong color?

An interesting corollary: the medium or mystic in his sensitive vibration-mechanism faces the danger of slaloming into alcoholism; one may almost call it an occupational disease: e.g., the medium Mr. Ford. Some of the foremost mediums have turned away from alcohol because the effects of the stimulant interfered with and misdirected their other vibrations. The Mexicans who administer the mushroom to their disciples prescribe in their ritual a minimum of seventy-two hours of total abstinence from alcohol, tea, coffee, sex, and any other stimulants before they tender this gift of the gods.

Certain cautions about the use of the mushroom are mentioned, for there may be a relationship here to addiction. All through the ages, the mystics have warned against the misuse of this power, for one may lose contact with reality or one may open up channels of energy which may destroy the man who is not yet ready for their use. In China, India, and Mexico, one approaches this ritual at certain times and receives prescribed amounts dictated by the needs of the individual. Here the doctor-priest determines the amount for each person. And certain warnings are given that must be followed in the pre-trance and trance state.

Are the alcoholic and the drug addict tuning in on the wrong wave length? Are the alcoholic and the drug addict tuning in on the right wave length, but using the wrong means to reach cosmic consciousness, samadhi, or nirvanah on the ladder of the mounting mystic experience? Are they trying to recapture the **Forgotten Language** without knowing it? Psychology, physiology, medicine fail to eradicate the cause of their trouble. Color must be used and vibrations remain as the only way if the experiments in missiles and physics provide any valid directives. The missile on the right frequency hits the target; the missile on the wrong frequency will go off in a completely different direction. Color vibration is the only cure for the alcoholic and the drug addict because this is the only road to clear up the jamming of the frequencies.

One may then ask, are alcohol and drug addictions diseases of the etheric body, not of the physical body? One final question, are the Indian mystics and the Tibetans correct in their description of the age as an eon of confusion that must be destroyed to be born again (Kalpa)? Let this thought be applied to the addicts today. Literal interpretation of this statement means that man must learn how to tune in on cosmic consciousness or else he will be destroyed by the atomic bombs, by flood, or by some other disaster, say the cyber-social revolution that modern society faces. Is this the reason for the rise of alcoholism in every country of the world? Can color reverse the process? The author says yes, if color is used correctly and if man tunes in on the proper vibration. Then the ceiling is unlimited.

Egypt: Contributions to Color Healing

In the Egyptian temples, archeologists found evidence of a special mode of construction where rooms were built so that the sun's rays were broken up into the seven colors of the spectrum and thus color was used as an aid to healing as well as for worship.

The healer would diagnose what color or colors the individuals lacked, and then the individual would bathe in the room with the color that was needed for the restoration of his health. Further, the mystery of the construction of the pyramids as being built upon true North, South, East, and West was used for their perfect relationship to the planets and to the forces of the universe.

The Egyptians as well as the Chinese were especially specific about their use of color, and they dramatized it by relating it to the various gods that they worshipped. They taught that the colors blue, yellow, and red were the activating forces of man's physical, mental and spiritual being. This belief the mystics also included in their philosophy. The blues or the chemical rays were most powerful in the morning and in the spring for germination and thus they had this power correspond with the Egyptian God Thoth who used colors to awaken the spiritual centers in the head. The yellow rays of Isis, most powerful at noon and in the summer, were responsible for stimulating man's mentality. The red heating rays of Osiris were the strongest in the afternoon and in the autumn, and they entered through the breath and gave man life. The Egyptians also used the technique of having the patient drink solarized water, and this practice has carried over among all peoples: Indians, Chinese, South American Indians, etc.

With regard to gems, the Egyptians used them for their color treatment, and gem therapy to this day continues to be practiced both in Egypt and in India. The theory underlying their use is that the gems are pure in color, are concentrated, and are of one hue; hence they are unadulterated in their effect on the body. When the gem is rotated, its rays are released. The theory then evolved not only among the Egyptians but also among other Eastern peoples that the planets influenced human behavior physically, psychologically, emotionally, and spiritually, and the gems have the same rays as the planets. Thus they represent the same influences as the planets do, but not as forcefully. It is interesting to note that the Egyptians, like the other nations of the time, would grind up the precious gems and use the powder as a curative. Here is reflected the modern doctrine of Isotopes.

The early Egyptians—like the Early Indians, Chinese, Japanese, Persians, Arabians, Peruvians, Guatamalians—were fully aware of the perceptual appeal of color and used it to a high degree in their religious ceremonies. Thus color was inter-related with perfumes. This practice of using perfumes became a very important part of Indian and Chinese practice; a whole ceremonial evolved about working the various mudras with perfumes being present to create a spiritual and mental rapport.

According to Roland, Hunt, the Annamite Kings of Indo-China used the knowledge of the faculties in their colorful burial tombs on the banks of the Sacred River of Perfumes. So here is seen a methodology that becomes associated with all the events of living and dying.

What a far cry this evolution spells from the state of prehistoric man. At this point the reader is reminded that anthropologists report prehistoric man could not see color[3]—he could see just black and white. The faculty to see color developed slowly and is still developing. Today we see two phenomena that are familiar: those who are color blind—a throw back to the past—and those who are gifted with extrasensory perception of color—like the clairvoyants. Perhaps in the space age, man will have to project his color sense in order to adjust to the challenges the universe thrusts upon him.

In a specific analysis of the beliefs of the Egyptians with regard to healing and color and how they put these beliefs into practice, one must stress their belief in incantations. From a review of the various Papyri with their report of various magical prayers and magical statements, the recitation of the incantation reminds one of the Buddha prayers that should be repeated about 900,000 times. Obviously the technique of repetition of an enchantment or prayer is the same—whether in ancient Egypt, in ancient India, or in ancient China: the technique to change a vibration and to cultivate another consciousness. If there were an imbalance, then work on a particular vibration and in one color as well as in one point of repeated mental view would restore the equilibrium. And they used their whole pantheon of Gods to develop this type of awareness—for a form of conditioning.

3. Man does not have to see or feel color to be affected by it.

Among the Egyptians, each family and almost each individual possessed a god or goddess, or a fetish who had a niche or a shrine in the household. This god or fetish was loved, respected, worshipped, consulted, and obeyed. Almost from the very beginning, the gods were divided into two classes: those representing the cosmic forces of nature: namely, the sun, the moon, the stars, the atmosphere, and the earth and those others projecting the tribal or official divinities of the "nomes" and the cities. Especially to be stressed, however, was the Solar Pantheon, for the Egyptians viewed the Sun from different views and with various names; and later they even combined various functions with their different interpretations of the Sun God.

In the famous city of Heliopolis, the sun God of the morning was Khepri, a winged beetle rising in the eastern sky; the natural sun of noon was Re; and the evening sun was Atum, who appeared as an old man tottering to his grave in the west. The moon Thoth was the eye of the sun-god.

The sun god was believed to be the ally and protector of the kings of Egypt who assumed the title of Re about the Fifth Dynasty. Every pharaoh thereafter claimed to be a divine incarnation and a bodily son of this god Re and the pharaoh often acted as the first priest and officiated at important ceremonies.

There were also great and powerful master spirits of evil: the serpent Apop who represented darkness and was spiritually opposed to Re. Each morning he fought with Re to prevent the rising of the sun; and although he was always defeated, he renewed the struggle daily to continue the darkness. To Seth, brother of Osiris and Isis and a helper of the dead, was attibuted the calamities that man was heir to.

According to the academicians, the Gods were responsible for healing and therefore the rules of healing were not subject to improvement by man.[4] To the author this type of generalization

---

4. Walter Addison Jayne, M.D., **The Healing Gods of Ancient Civilizations,** N.Y. University Books, Inc., 1925, 1962, p. 34: "It was the duty of rulers to continue the work of the good gods who had founded Egypt...and since healing had been devised by the divinities, it was not subject to improvement by man."

made by the scholars is as "phony" as the story about the identity of the wife of the "unknown soldier." If this theory is true, then there could only be one healing god who gave to man a set of perfect healing rules at the beginning of time.

With regard to healing, the written records describing these processes are the Papyri, and the most important are listed below:

1. Kahun Papyrus, dating from about 2000 B.C.
2. The Edwin Smith Papyrus, dating from about 1600 B.C. This is superior to the Ebers Papyrus and it is claimed to be, "... the oldest nucleus of scientific knowledge in the world and contains incomparably the most important body of medical knowledge which has survived to us from ancient Egypt or from the ancient Orient anywhere." It deals with surgery and internal medicine covering the upper half of the body.[5]
3. The Hearst Medical Papyrus between the 12 and 18 Dynasties.
4. Berlin Papyrus from about 1600 B.C.
5. Ebers Papyrus from about 1552 B.C.; this has 110 pages; it shows skill, knowledge, and a systematic arrangement of **materia medica** and appears to be a compilation of several smaller works. It deals with medicine, surgery, prescriptions, incantations, and enchantments.
6. The Greater Berlin or the Brugsch Papyrus, dating about 1350 B.C.
7. The London Medical Papyrus, dating about 1000 B.C.
8. Lyden Papyrus.
9. Turin Papyrus.
10. Harris Magical etc., Papyrus and Mother and Child Papyrus.

One example for proof of how the Egyptian healer applied his precepts is found in Prescription Number XXXI of the Kahun Papyrus where obviously the doctor-healer knew some method to determine the sex of the unborn child or else he used a form of the

---

5. **Ibid.,** pp. 35-38. The reader is reminded that the Dead Sea Scrolls, which were discovered after this Jayne book was published, are reputed to contain more information about religion and healing than the Smith and the Ebers Papyrus. According to Chinese authorities, acupuncture is older.

confusion technique to prevent information from getting into the hands of the uninitiated, a device used by the occultists to this very day:

> If thou seest her face green...she will
> bring forth a male (?) child, but if
> thou seest things upon her eyes
> she will not bear ever.[6]

The Egyptian literature affords little information concerning their views or disease. But they never resigned themselves to the idea that death was inevitable. Life once begun should continue indefinitely. Disease was regarded as a visitation of demons, jealous gods, animals, and enemies who gained entry into the body by supernatural means, in an unguarded moment, through the eyes, ears, mouth, and nose. Let the reader substitute the word "microbes" for the words or phrases of "demons, enemies, gods, and animals," and the theory of allopathic medicine is illustrated. Egyptian belief coincides with the modern practice of medicine as reported in the various historical texts. It is the author's opinion, however, that the Egyptian priests and priestesses gave out information for "public consumption," but practiced in their "inner sanctum" or behind their "closed doors" a set of "rational" precepts of healing that were based on natural laws of physiology, psychology, and the science of the mind.

The Egyptians further believed in lucky and unlucky days, practiced "sanitation"—personal and social—and also taught what is today termed the "science of nutrition." The general population wore amulets to keep away evil spirits, the most popular being the "Eyes of Horus." If the wearing of an amulet for its psychological healing power is called a fetish, one then asks these questions:

Is not the belief in an injection to ward off disease a fetish? Is not the belief in the power of vaccination also a modern fetish? A number of authorities place no credence in vaccination. The ancient Chinese and Indians practiced vaccination thousands of

6. **Ibid.**, p. 36.

years ago before the West was even aware of germs and then discontinued the practice because they concluded it was valueless and led to an iatrogenic disease called vaccina.

There is no denying that the Egyptian priest understood the full power of suggestion in healing exactly as the modern physician does and as the Madison Avenue topflight advertising agency executes. Did the Egyptian healer allow the common man to believe in the fetish or amulet and rely upon the theories and rules of sanitation? Did he not understand how the vibrations of the colors in the materials used affected the human body? Color was used in Heliopolis, the City of Light. The Egyptians knew the tides, the movement of the planets, the Nile and its overflow. Was the worship of the sun, the giver of color in the city of Heliopolis, accidental or deliberate? To what extent was the credulous acceptance of the amulet and the fetish also a form of mental suggestion, employing hypnosis?

Egyptian medicine was at its best in diagnosis and in physiological speculations. The Egyptians practiced surgery but their **materia medica,** on the other hand, remained permanently under the influence of magical conceptions. They studied nature's laws. These facts, intermingled with the mysteries of their faith, were not divulged to their contemporaries; the writing of the classical authors living in Greek and Roman times bears testimony to their failure in comprehending what they had observed and what was reported to them. Even to the Egyptians themselves, the knowledge was restricted to those within the inner circle, those within the mystery, as it is limited today among the Mexican Indians; for example, the Zapotecs—where the healing information is passed down orally to the initiated and to the select few.

The Egyptians were responsible for laying down the ground work of careful observation, precepts which are the foundation blocks of western empiric medicine. The Greeks and the Romans, although having the superficial understanding, borrowed freely and very frequently without acknowledging their indebtedness to the Egyptians. Plato is said by Clemens Alexandricus to have remarked concerning the Greeks, that "Whatever we receive from the barbarians we improve and perfect."

Of the many gods listed in the Egyptian cosmography, only those projecting a color-healing function in theory or practice will be listed:

Khonsu—son of Ammon and Mut. He was the messenger of the Gods in the form of the moon. Known for his miraculous cures, he was credited with the ability to effect cures by substitution, lending the healing forces from his own "soul energy"; for example, his SA—to an image or double; "Bestowing upon it . . .[7] its protective fluids at four intervals."

Neith was one of the most ancient deities in the Egyptian pantheon; originating in the First Dynasty, she presided over the city of Sais. In the Delta area of Egypt, she was known as the Goddess Sais. Associated with the theology of Atun-Re at Heliopolis, who is the Father-God, she was called the Mother-Goddess. She was the mighty mother who gave birth to Re and was called the Great Lady, the Lady of Heaven, and the queen of the Gods. The term Self-born or Self-Produced was applied to her. She is said to have brought forth Re without the aid of her husband (virgin birth). The Greeks have equated her with Athena; the Festival of Lamps (not Chanukah) celebrated annually at Sais was famous and renowned throughout the Ancient Worlds; she was esteemed for being the Goddess of Fertility and of Childbirth.

Serapis or **Osor-Hap** was introduced into the Egyptian pantheon by Ptolemy 1 with the intention of establishing a God in whose worship the Greeks could join at a common shrine and who would give distinction to his reign. The Egyptians received Serapis reluctantly, and he never became popular with the people. Serapis assumed the title of Osiris, the Nile God, and then he became known as the God of the Underworld and the Judge of the Dead; Serapis absorbed all the functions of these Gods although the original ceremonial rites were changed to accommodate to Serapis' assumption of the new role. Isis was associated with Serapis in cultic worship by Ptolemy. To some authorities, Serapis

---

7. The nape of the neck. This is the same as F.M. Alexander's term primary control in the Atlantoid-Occipital area.

became Baal or Belzepur (Belzebub) of Babylonia who is equated occasionally with Zeus by some people. To others, Serapis was the great Babylonian healing deity Ea of Erieu, under his common title Sar-Apsi, King of the Watery Deep with his Dream Oracle; Bouche-Leclercq remarks that "... under his name was collected the debris of numerous personalities worn out by time." His cult spread rapidly throughout Greece were it became a powerful rival to that of Asklepios (Aesculapius). It also spread to Rome and its provinces until his temples where destroyed when Theodosius suppressed paganism.

Isis or **Eset** was one of the most popular and also one of the oldest goddesses of Egypt. Worshipped as a protective deity, she was the daughter of Pueb and Nut and the sister of Osiris, Horus the elder, and Nephthys, wife of Osiris, and the mother of the child Horus. She is one of the chief divinities of the underworld, the kingdom of the dead, and, as consort of Osiris, appears with him in the Judgment scenes. Represented by Maat—the Egyptian word for Judgment—she is called the Goddess of the West as a result of her identification with Hat-Hor. Also equated with Astarte, Aphrodite, Demeter, and Persephone, she is associated with many of the important myths of Egyptian religion, and she gained her unusual powers as a magician by means of outwitting the supreme god Re and learning his secret name; thereby, she earned the name of Weret-Hike—She Who Is Great of Magic. Isis is a healing divinity of the first rank and cared for her people— especially the children.

1-M-Hotep—He Who Comes in Peace: He was the astrologer for the priests of Re and was renowned for his wise epigrams. Being a patron of learning, of scholars, and of physicians, he was deified after the Persian period (525 B.C.) and elevated to the rank of a healing God by becoming the son of Ptah and of Sekhmet. He was the physician of God and of man: "The God who sent sleep to those who were suffering and in pain and those who were afflicted with any kind of disease formed his especial care. He was the divinity of physicians and of all those who were occupied with the meaningful signs of medicine and of magic."

Ptah was one of the primeval deities called "The Very Great God" who also represented wisdom. As the creator of Gods and of the World, he was thus a therapeutic divinity of great renown and his temples at Memphis were famous for the remarkable cures he effected (The Lourdes of Egypt).

Sekhmet or The Lady of the Lamp was pictured with the head of a lionness usually surrounded by a solar disk with Uraeus. As consort and female counterpart of Ptah, she represented fire and the intense destroying heat of the sun. Re gave her the function of destroying the enemies of god and of mankind. She did her job so well that she was called the lady of pestilence. In Egyptian language, she fell in love with the blood of man and had to be forcible restrained in her lust for drinking blood. She was also a therapeutic deity, and her priests were renowned in the curative arts as expert bone setters. (Compare with Indian Kali or Durga.)

Thoth, Thout, or **Tohuti** was the Moon God who spoke the words that created the world. He was the God of Wisdom through whom all mental gifts were imparted to man and the possessor of every kind of knowledge; as the founder of the social order, he devised the sacred ritual for proper approach to the deities with prayers and sacrifices: among other things, he was the inventor of language, numbers, the arts and the sciences— including astronomy, architecture, medicine, and botany. Intimately associated with the myths of the Osirian cycle, he is a powerful patron of physicians. His temple at Hermopolis was probably the greatest healing temple of ancient Egypt. The Gods equated him with Hermes as Psychopompos.

Iran (Persia): Contributions to Color Healing

In ancient Iran, as in other countries of the time, medical doctrines and practices were under the control of the priests who played the dual role of healer and priest. The sacred text of the ancient Iranians was destroyed during the invasion of Alexander the Great, and the approximate third that has survived forms the basis of the scriptures of the Parsis of India and of their co-religionists, the Gebirs, in Persia. The **Avesta,** ascribed by tradition to have been written by Zoroaster himself, treats of the teachings of Zarathustra or Zoroaster, the legends, the moral and civil law, the liturgy as well as the ritual and the cosmology, which flourished about 1000 B.C. Its specific **Law against the Demons**—called the **Vendidad**—mentions disease quite frequently and its chapters twenty to thirty two are almost wholly concerned with medical matters.

The main feature of Zoroastrianism is an essential monotheism with an apparent dualism. The principle of good is represented by Ahura Mazda or Ormazd, the omniscient creator of the universe and of all good things. The principle of evil is Angra Mainyu or Ahriman, the Enemy Spirit, who, ignorant and shortsighted, created darkness, sin, disease and evil of every kind. Those two are in mortal combat, and man engages in the struggle, by aiding the one or opposing the other according to his moral attitudes. This conflict continues until the world will undergo an ordeal that will eventually eliminate evil and purify the universe.

The Ahura Mazda and the Ahriman of the Zoroastrians further indicate a belief in the continuous balancing of the two forces of life—a belief somewhat similar to the belief of the Chinese in the Yin and the Yang forces that are opposed to each other, but never antagonistic. And color is the healing reconciliation between them.

Many of the Iranian myths date from the period of Indo-Iranian unity; and if these stories are compared with those of the Indian **Vedas,** one sees a marked similarity in theme, plot, and form; only personalities and details are changed of names and places.

In the consideration of disease, it is interesting to note that diseases were named after particular demons who were governed by the quasi-dualism which rules the cosmos. Since disease was regarded as an attack by or as a possession by spirits of evil, the power of good spirits had to be invoked to secure relief. Sin was a spiritual malady and disease a bodily malady; the first, a breach of the moral order and the second, of the physical, but both resulting from pollution, in one form or another. This pollution therefore had to be removed by some rite or act of purification. Their methods thus included invocations, hymns, and conjuration often in conjunction with natural remedies administered with other rites and ceremonies. Airyaman, it was believed, created 99,999 diseases, and Ormazd, acting through Zoroaster, revealed to man how to counteract the afflictions of Angra Mainyu. The cure was effected by Amesha, Spensa or Haurvatat—who signified Wholeness and Health—through the medium of the physician. The **Avesta** has several categories of healing art as the following quotation reveals wherein surgery (knife) is the lowest form of healing, a concept also reflected in the mythology of India, China and Japan:

> "One health by righteousness, one health
> by the law, one health by the knife;
> one health by plants; one health by the
> (holy) text."

The Iranian made no distinction between curing man and curing animals. The same principles and procedures applied to both and the same gods were appealed to. Mention is made, in passing, of five Iranian healing gods.

Airyaman was a god of the Indo-Iranian period. After the Holy Texts failed, Ahura Mazda called for his co-operation in expelling disease and death. He did his job so well through the rites of purification that the 99,999 diseases ceased. His special prayer was the most powerful of all divine mantras in healing. Airyaman's middle Persian name means friend—the modern word Irman means quest—and his prayer has its Indian counterpart in the **Aditya Aryaman.**

Aredvi Sura Anahita meant lofty, mighty, a spotless lady, a divinity of the waters, especially of the mystic river Aredvi. Associated with Mithra and the only other deity mentioned besides Ahura Mazda in the Achamenian inscriptions, she dwelt among the stars guarding all holy creation, granting the prayers of the righteous, but rejecting the adherents of Azhi Dahaka. She had a chariot drawn by four white steeds who represented respectively wind, rain, cloud and sleet. In Greek mythology, she is associated with Artemis and occasionally with Aphrodite. Her cult was spread throughout the ancient world where she was called the Great Mother of the Asiatic people.

Hoama was the Iranian counterpart of the Vedic Soma. He was an Iranian deity from primeval time and appeared in terrestrial form as the yellow Hoama used in the Indo-Iranian sacrifices. According to the **Avesta,** the juice of this plant was first extracted by Mithra from a health-giving and invigorating herb brought by the birds from lofty Haraiti Mount Elburz; in its sacred character, it became the ceremonial drink which gave strength and life to man. This drink was prepared by the priests with elaborate prayers, prescribed ritual and significant ceremonies. (Was this the mushroom?)

Mithra of the **Vedas** was an Iranian deity of great antiquity. He was identified with the all-seeing sun although among the Iranians, he was the divinity of righteousness and of the plighted word, the protector of justice, and the defender of truth and righteousness in the struggle of man against Ahriman. He was famous as a moral arbitrator struggling against the forces of evil to redeem mankind. This eternal contest was symbolized by the slaying of the bull as a symbol of regeneration. Other ceremonies included communion with bread and wine, ointments of honey for the consecration of the body; these were, in reality, mystical remedies for the healing of the body and the sanctification of the soul.

Little is known of the ritual of the Iranian worship of Mithra, but his cult in the Occident became associated with mysticism, occultism, magic and astrology, much of which was believed to have been injected by the Chaledonians. The popular and powerful cult of Mithra then spread rapidly from Asia Minor to Greece and throughout the Roman Empire. The appeal of Chaledonian occultism and the mysterious sciences of the Orient encountered bitter opposition from the party supporting Christianity, and this religious struggle continued as late as the fifth century. It was a popular sight for the Romans to see astrologers who were followers of Mithra spend the nights on the tops of the Roman Towers or the Mithra magicians practice their "mysteries" on the banks of the Tiber.

Yima represented the setting sun as well as the first man, and thus the chief of the souls of the departed. Ancient Indo-Iranian stories recount the story of Yama, the twin of the **Veda,** but Yima of the Iranian stories appears in the **Avesta** as the son of Vivahvant and the hero of one of the early myths of the expansion of the world. In his golden age, he ruled at a time when food and drink were plentiful and when there was no age nor death.

Yima committed a sin by giving man forbidden food and also by yielding to falsehood. For this he lost his kingly realm and glory and was slain by the dragon Azhi Dahaka, a monster created by Ahriman with three jaws, three heads, and six eyes, and on whose shoulders grew two snakes from the kisses of Ahriman. Azhi Dahaka's reign was evil and malignant so that he was finally overpowered by the hero Thraetaona Faradium, the Indian counterpart of whom is Traitana. Thraetaona Faradium was a great healer, and his favors were sought against the itch, against fever, and against two unknown diseases.

A brief word here about the Persian Unani system, which stands next to the Indian system of Ayurveda. It is a medical system advocating accurate pulse examination, excellent diet and effective medicines. That Unani developed so well was the response to the autocratic emperors who demanded from the Hakims, their term for doctors, on pain of dire consequences, quick relief without any kind of restriction on diet or bad habits. The Hakims had to develop a system of sure medical relief and accurate diagnosis.

India: Contributions to Color Healing: Eight Tenets

1. Man is identified with the creative forces of the universe that are seen through the visible colors of the spectrum and the invisible colors; man therefore is primarily god-like and has a potential for good.
2. Man is never regarded as evil. He is seen as part of the omnipresent, omniscient, and omnipotent forces of the universe and through developing his self-awareness of his consciousness of himself and his identity with the universe, he

comes to a state of liberation (Samadhi or Cosmic Consciousness.) There is therefore no concept of evil or guilt. All men have the potential for god-like evolution if they wish to expand through meditation and concentration. They can take one life time or many life times the doctrine of reincarnation here implicit in their culture, a belief alien to the Western mind.

3. They base their evolution on man's awareness from the within to the without. Man goes within himself in his meditation, and he discovers the reaches and the powers of himself are not of himself, but are a part of the cosmic forces of the universe which he individualizes in himself through his living processes: breathing, etc. Thus the key to healing is from within to the without. This precept differs from the Western man's medical view-point where the stress has been from the without to the within. Western man has only now developed a theory of psychology and psychoanalysis, ideas which are thousands of years old in India.

4. Their work in meditation and developing of the self leading to the liberated state of Samadhi (or Nirvana or Cosmic Consciousness) led them to promulgate the idea that there is no dichotomy of body, mind or spirit and thus they evolved their theory of the way in which the chakras worked on the body. The chakras, in Western terminology, are the endocrine glands and the nervous system. The Indians interpreted these centers as dynamos of energy—physical, psychic, and spiritual and associated each center with colors vital to the health and well-being of the total man. Western science has subjected these glands to scientific study since 1910, but in India, this study is thousands of years old.

5. The Indians have made use of the auras, the electro-magnetic field force which surrounds the body and which has been photographed. These relate to the theory of the seven bodies which radiate the seven colors of the spectrum.

This theory of the auras, the seven bodies of man, and the mudras as well as the perfumes is even projected in their mythology which is used to teach people, among other things, the principles of color healing and self-awareness. Mention will be made of the **Kurma Purana** with the "Grandfather" simplification and the works of **Ayurveda** to see how the Indians have projected the story of the basic five elements of nature and the vital forces in the Tridoshas as they affect the senses, the colors in the body, the colors in the universe, the movements of the planets as well as the forces that move the planets. What moves the individual also moves the celestial spheres.

7. To the Indian, color is both an objective and subjective influence, a concept not fully accepted by the Westerners.
8. The Indian philosophy accepts the clairvoyant's vision as "scientific;" Western man regards such impressions and reports as purely subjective and tends to eschew them or to regard them as part of the lunatic fringe.

Chakras

Each Chakra is an active pulsating vortex of vital energy, with its outer edge lying on the surface of the body. The central swirl of each vortex sweeps into the body in a long stalk that makes contact with vital currents in the spinal fluid which flows in the marrow of the spinal cord and is carried to the organism by the nervous system. Vitality flowing along the spinal cord discharges itself through these same central stalks out to the mouth of the chakra and to the outer aura. It looked like a lotus flower, the stem rooted in the spinal cord and the flower blossoming on the upper surface of the etheric body. According to the Indians, man has twelve senses, not five, which are controlled by the chakras through the nerves and endocrine system. They are the organs by which thought and feeling first register at the emotional and mental level and directly affect the physical body. But their action is specialized. Each one reacts to and draws into the body a special current of vital energy from the environment. Briefly stated, they control the body, the mind, and the psyche; they regulate the whole functioning of the body—such as sex growth, metabolism, circulation, elimination, etc.

According to ancient Indian doctrine, they are intimately related to the sevenfold bodies of man (Organic, Nervous, Etheric, Astral, Mental, Causal and Buddic) which interpenetrate each other because of their discriminating subtle etheric and atomic structure. The chakras may be said not only to cover the material constitution and function of the endocrine glands but also to comprise the energy functions and the psychic effects. These seven are really functioning dynamos of energy and all have their color equivalents as a portion of their healing aspects. The Indians also stated that the ego has the seven chakras which act also as the spiritual centres to activate the endocrine glands of the physical body; they believe that man must be treated as one unit: body, mind, and soul or spirit.

Any malfunction of the chakras affects the particular gland, and the whole endocrine system is then out of balance. The Indians further believed that the color indigo controls the psychic currents of the subtle bodies and governs the chakra in the middle of the forehead; that is, the spiritual or the third eye. Thus color becomes a healing reconciliation among the various forces of the body. If there is an imbalance in either direction, too great a materiality or too great a spirituality, ill health may result. Mystical nonsense? Perhaps; but here is found Selye's theory of stress (G-A-S).

There is an interchange of fluids, vibrations and currents among the chakras through the channel called Kundalini, the Sacred Serpent power, which has positive and negative vibrations and which is the basis of life (personality). The earth's currents enter the body through the foot chakra, the left being positive and the right being negative. The knee chakra reduces the currents according to the body's needs. The root and sacral chakras combine the earth's currents and reverse the polarity. The new positive current flows along the spinal cord through the splenic and heart chakras. It continues until it reaches the throat chakra where the second combining of positive and negative currents occurs. The negative current in the meantime ascends to the throat chakra through the kidney, spleen, and stomach. From the throat chakra the newly transformed vibrations, which are bipolar, divide and descend into the hand chakras. Negative current flows into the right hand and positive into the left hand.[8] Other currents flow into the mental body mainly through the intuitive chakra.

In general these currents meet and remain in the throat chakra. Function is slow or impeded in most of humanity. In certain individuals, this current mixes with the high tension currents of the mental body and becomes polarized. The result is that there is an enormously high number of revolutions for the chakra concerned. The slower the movement of the chakra, the denser is the mass of man and the more physical becomes the individual; the slower the flow, the denser the mass, the less spiritual is the person. Conversely, the more rapid the flow or movement of the chakra, the less dense the man, the more spiritual is the individual[9] (is this an explanation of Samadhi, Nirvana, or Cosmic Consciousnss?). At a certain rate of vibration, the Holy Light or a spiritual force manifests itself as recorded in religious literatures. This is the light seen by the clairvoyants.

Movement of the chakras takes place clockwise; the rate of revolution depends on the individual's evolution. There are cases where the individual chakra is an anomaly and turns in a counter-

8. The Chinese accept the left side as positive in the male and right side as negative and the reverse in the female. Eeman's view is that the right side is positive in right-handed individuals and the left side is positive in left-handed individuals. In Indian mythology, the statue of the Siva-Parvathi, an androgynous figure, has the right side as male Siva and the left side as female Parvathi.

9. The author wishes to comment on death and immortality without any references to Wordsworth's "Ode on Intimations of Immortality." At the moment of birth, the infant emits an indigo color—the mark of the fastest vibration and the shortest wave length. It is at this moment that the uncorrupted being is the most spiritual. As he grows older, his vibrations change in his travel from the spiritual to the physical pathway and the shift is from the more frequent to the less frequent vibrations and from shorter to longer wave lengths. When he approaches the red end, he is on the road out of the forty-ninth for he is being "burnt-up." Man's life, it may be said, is the visible spectrum for this is the color ranging from indigo to red. When he leaves the road of the visible spectrum or approaches the red end, the point of exhaustion called death is reached. But THE PROCESS IS ALWAYS REVERSIBLE IF ONE EXCLUDES ACCIDENTS. The spiritual exit is by way of indigo.

clockwise direction. This produces imbalance in the etheric body and causes all kinds of nervous diseases. Schizophrenia is the result of an imbalance in the chakra.

The Indians were aware that breathing, sound, color, jewels and electrical gadgets could affect the chakras: for example, the vowels affect the following organs—O the stomach; E the liver and gall bladder; U the sexual organs; I the spleen; A the heart.

Compare with Sir Lawrence Bragg's statement that we are "right-handed corkscrews." It is interesting to note that among the thirty-two principles of beauty associated with Buddha, one aspect is that his hair was to grow and curl in a right-handed manner and the hair to be screw-turned to the right (special reference is made to the stone carved statue Gal Vihara—of the reclining Buddha found in the Polonnaruwa ruins in Ceylon).

Because color is perceptual, it influences the physical and the higher sense and can heal the physical and the higher consciousness. Thus the Indians assumed that color therapy could be applied on the physical, psychological, and spiritual levels. And this they taught.

1. Root Center chakra (Muladhara or Mooladhara Chakra-Coccygeal—Equivalent of Sacral Plexus); nourished by yellow.

    This lies above the anus, but below the root of the sex organs. Sushumna opens here and Kundalini enters through this chakra. The color is yellow: the element is earth; the sense of smell is associated with it as well as the feet or organs of action. The phenomenon of accumulation is associated with it (4 petals; 4 letters). This is a double chakra composed of two centers, located over the sexual organs of both sexes in the area of the coccyx (lesbianism and homosexuality are to be treated at this point). This double chakra is unipolar instead of bipolar. The coccygeal and the neck chakras are both known as the "Death chakras."

    To some Western occult groups who have combined Christianity with Eastern mysticism, this chakra, called the Fundamental Chakra, is symbolized frequently by a cross as its four rays form that shape. They claim that this chakra accumulates energy like an electric battery and stores the energy of life. The cross here is regarded as the emblem of the positive and negative poles, action and reaction, masculine and feminine—all of which are imperative to life. To these occultists the symbol implies creativity, procreation, origin of life, the father-mother principles, etc.

The author here presents one interpretation of what he calls a mixture of Oriental and Occidental philosophy which turns out to be a Chop Suey wherein Eastern ideas were bastardized by Western infiltrations of Christianity. Christ, instead of being a young God and being blended with the beliefs of East and West, becomes the most powerful God. They substituted the terms Christ-like force for Buddhistic or Taoistic force. The reader is cautioned against this trap. No effort will be made to repeat this type of correlation for any of the other charkras except to warn the reader about the last, the seventh chakra. Under no circumstances should the reader confuse this chakra with the Golden Light cultivated by the Taoists.

Treat here with yellow for diseases of the blood and liver. Treat for febrile diseases, smallpox, boils, ringworms, inflammations, bleeding for any cause, bladder trouble and toothaches.

2. Support of Life-Breath chakra (Swadhishatana or Chakra-splenic-Equivalent of prostatic plexus); nourished by orange.

This significant chakra is actually composed of secondary chakras that are most important for the secretion of the ductless glands and the organs, such as stomach, liver and gall bladder. It is the stress chakra. This lies at the end of the root of the sex organs; it is connected with the crescent and with the element of water. Its color is white and it is associated with the phenomenon of contraction (6 petals).

The splenic chakra has as its function that of drawing in a current of physical prana. It is composed of a vitality globule formed in sunlight and ultra-violet light and closely associated with pure oxygen. It is discharged along the nervous system flowing along the myelin sheath of the nerve, not through the fibres, and is distributed to all parts of the body; the surplus and used particles then flow out through the skin and help form the emanation. This becomes the aura and not the halo, as mistakenly described by some people. Everybody has an aura, but few have a halo, which is the sign of spirituality.

For physical health the intake of physical prana is of immense importance. Prana is not drawn in through the lungs but its intake is directly associated with breathing. The breathing rhythm induces greater activity of the splenic chakra which focuses intake of physical prana or vitality.[10]

Treat here for diseases of the bladder, mental illness, fever, polyurea, tuberculosis, diarrhea, edema, colic, colitis, eyes, anemia, diabetes, and cancer.

3. Lotus of the Navel chakra (Manipura or Haripuraka Chakra-Equivalent to the Solar Plexus); nourished by red.

This is found in the region of the navel; its color is red and it is connected with the triangle and with the element of fire. It is associated with the phenomenon of sight, the anus and expansion and affects the sympathetic nervous system and the emotions (10 petals).

Diseases treated are circulatory, heart, all osseous ailments, facial paralysis, gout, and headaches.

4. Centre of Unstruck Sound chakra (Anahata Chakra-Equivalent to Cardiac Plexus); nourished by violet.

This is the seat of the vital breath and is connected with the hexagon: its element is air and is associated with touch, with feeling and with the phenomenon of thought. Blue is associated with it and the spleen (12 petals and 12 letters).

Treat diseases of the nervous system, skin, hysteria, deafness, joints, and constipation.

5. Centre of Great Purity chakra (Vishudha Chakra—Equivalent to Pharyngeal Plexus). Double Chakra; nourished by indigo.

10. See AdeVaide Gardner, **Vital Magnetic Healing.**

This is located in the throat and is connected with the spiral: its element is ether and it is associated with the mouth. Its color is bluish-green and is associated with the phenomenon of space (16 letters and 16 petals).

Treat diseases of gonads, lymph, skin, senility, diabetes, infections, and low blood pressure.

6.   Center of Command chakra (Aina or Ajna Chakra Equivalent to Cavernous Plexus); nourished by blue.

This is located between the two brows; its color is white and it is associated with the mind: arch principle of existence and the universal subtle body. Above this, lies the principal aperture where the three **subtle** arteries unite: Ida, blue in color; Pinagala, red in color; and Sushumna, extremely red, most brilliantly red. Ida and Pinagala both start at the coccygeal chakra in the coccyx; Ida, as female principle, rises on the left side of the spinal cord; Pinagala, as the male principle, rises on the right side of the spinal cord. Both travel twistingly upward from caudal to cephalic area; they alternate from left to right and from right to left in a corkscrew fashion. Both then unite with Sushumna on the top of the head (these are the nerves of the subtle bodies, not of the physical body, although they follow the neural pathways).

Treat diseases of throat, emotions, paralysis, liver, obesity, vomiting, cold, and tumors.

7.   Lotus of a Thousand Petals or Coronary[11] chakra (Sahasrara Chakra. Controller of all chakras. Equivalent to the Pituitary or Cerebral Cortex); nourished by green.

This is located at the crown of the head or in the brain. It is said that when active, it is the most brilliant of all the chakras, for it appears to possess all the colors of the spectrum. Though it is called the Lotus of a Thousand Petals, it is supposed to possess only nine hundred and sixty petals. In its centre is a shape like a flower with twelve petals—all in a golden hue. Supposedly it is the chakra that increases in size as the intellect expands.

11. See Swami Vishnudevananda, **The Complete Illustrated Book of Yoga,** N.Y., Julian Press, 1960, pp. 292-4.

It is interesting to note that Brahma is often represented with this chakra on his head—a form of a crown with its nine hundred and sixty rays to symbolize the intellectual wisdom of the rulers. It became a custom for rulers to wear crowns as symbols of learning and wisdom. Is this origin to be found in the Coronary Chakra of Sahasrara?

Treat emotional diseases, vision, and ulcers.

Table 1: The Seven Major Chakras and the Body

CHAKRA	REGION INFLUENCED	GLAND AFFECTED	SPINAL CONTACT APPROXIMATE
Sacral	Pelvis and spleen	Gonads, pituitary	Base of spine
Splenic	Left side of abdomen	Endocrines	First lumbar
Solar plexus	Upper abdominal cavity	Adrenal	Eighth dorsal
Heart	Thorax	Thymus	Eighth cervical
Throat	Throat, base of nose, upper thorax	Thymus, thyroid	Third cervical
Brow	Basal ganglion, mid and hind brain	Pituitary	First cervical
Cranium	Master chakra	All	Atlas

In addition to the above seven chakras there are others; the most important are listed below.

8. Foot chakra is located on the sole of the foot; it absorbs the electric and other currents of the earth into the body of man.
9. Knee chakra acts as a transformer regulating the amount of current to enter the body.
10. Hand chakra absorbs the radio-active waves, a fact which may explain the healing power of the laying on of the hands.

Table 2:
The Fifteen Chakras—Cosmic and Color Relations

NUMBER	NAME	VALUE	PLANET	COLOR
1 and 2	Foot	8	Jupiter	Lilac
3 and 4	Knee	6	Saturn	Grey
5	Root	5	Mars	Red
6	Sacral	3	Saturn	Purple
7	Spleen	6	Earth	Green
8	Gallbladder	3	Saturn	Dark Green
9	Stomach	9	Moon	Dark Blue
10	Heart	3	Sun	Gold
11 and 12	Hand	16	Mercury	Yellow
13	Neck	3	Saturn	Dark Grey
14	Throat	7	Venus	Light Blue
15	Will or Intuition	3	Saturn	Dark Grey
		72		

Color, Seven Notes of the Scale, Seven Visible Colors of the Spectrum as Seven Subtle Healing Bodies

Indian writings revealed the belief that color and music played a vital part in the evolution of the seven subtle bodies of man. The seven colors of the visible spectrum and the seven notes of the scale also had their effect on the seven bodies, especially on the physical, emotional, and mental planes. They observed that the purer the color, the finer the tones, the greater the effect on the body.

As part of their philosophy, they said that the body was composed of air, water, minerals and warmth and that the substance of the soul was color. Color was as necessary to the soul as air to the body. Thus to them, color became the bridge of life by which one crossed the physical and emotional into the spiritual. Color was the healing reconciliation of all these levels by which man fused with the cosmic powers of the universe and became one with these limitless and eternal forces.

For this reason it is important to remember that they used color in healing on all levels of being and that these seven chakras or glandular centres, as described in Western terminology, are keyed to the seven colors of the spectrum. For those who do not or cannot believe, one may interpolate here that the Ohm meter and other instruments measure the electrical potential of these chakras.

India: The Auras

One school of Indian philosophy states:

1. That in the carnate state, man's ego is a blue light; as it descends towards incarnation, it appears as a yellow spark; on entering the physical body, it has a red vibration.
2. That man is composed of seven subtle bodies surrounding and interpenetrating the physical body; and that the magnetic and electrical radiations from these bodies compose the aura.
3. That each subtle body has an aura of its own which has its own distinct color and sound.
4. That these color radiations show the evolution of the soul and the state of health for each body.

It is the author's opinion that if all the colors of the minor auras are in harmony, the total individual is in health. If there is disharmony in one or more of the bodies, man has disease. He further maintains that the nerves are the sending and receiving apparatus for these subtle bodies and the messages are transmitted over the same nerve at different frequencies. Parkinson and Muscular Dystrophy, to name a few diseases, are not diseases of the physical body, although reflected in it, but are diseases of the etheric double. It is at the point of disharmony or at the auric level that one determines the disease; the names and the symptoms are not important in themselves as the cause is the same for each and the cure is restoration of harmony.

Everything one does affects the aura for better or for worse— like a marriage. Disease is nothing more than an imbalance in the vibration of the aura which is reflected in a change of color and in the physical body; this change is reflected in the nervous system as well as in the endocrine glands. The Indian physician uncontaminated by Western healing used to treat the physical body and the other subtle bodies as well. The method or technique varied—yoga, meditation, suggestion, color or any combination of these four approaches. In conclusion, it may be added that sometimes two or more auras can be seen. The one nearest the body is striated and called the inner aura; the other one, a wide amorphous part, is called the outer aura, as Kilmer reported. The space between the inner aura and the body is called the **etheric double.**

In ill health, the aura frequently contains more yellow than normally is its characteristic, and the yellow becomes pronounced in areas of local disturbances. This yellow is usually seen in patches in the midst of a blue complementary color band.

In a healthy person, the color of the complementary color band will be alike or nearly so on both sides of the body. But in illness, one side may be darker than the other, the dark part usually lying over the affected part of the body. The affected part, however, may cause the complementary color band to appear lighter instead of darker. Sometimes, a lighter or darker patch on the color band will occasionally take the shape of an organ or part of one. Smaller patches almost always point to the location of some pain or tenderness. Frequently a different colored spot will appear on the band, a spot that indicates the location of a previously sore spot. This need not indicate anything abnormal.

India: Color—ROYGBIV Applied to Man and to Cosmos—The PRISM

The **Kurma Purana,**[12] a writing sacred to the Hindus, describes the Creator as "Grandfather", a figure composed of rays of limitless color-variety, rays which pervade everything in the universe and rays which are endowed with the same power as the Creator whom they represent. The seven colors of the spectrum are the best of these colors because they form the matrices of the seven planets and are related to the seven days of the week, which are named for the planets in the following table:[13]

Table 3[14a]

DAY	TASTE	PLANET	GEM	COLOR	ELEMENT	SYMBOL	POLARITY
Sunday	Pungent	Sun	Ruby	Red	Fire	R	Negative
Monday	Astringent	Moon	Pearl	Orange	Water	O	Positive
Tuesday	Bitter	Mars	Coral	Yellow	Fire	Y	Negative
Wednesday	All six tastes	Mercury	Emerald	Green	Water	G	Positive
Thursday	Sweet	Jupiter	Moonstone	Blue	Air	B	Neutral
Friday	Sour	Venus	Diamond	Indigo	Water	I	Positive
Saturday	Saline	Saturn	Sapphire	Violet	Air	V	Neutral

[14a] A fuller explanation of Chinese organ interrelationships on pp. 93–97 complements the Indian views. Only the Chinese incorporated into their daily practice the ebb and flow in the body of the various energy channels known as meridians which have polarity, elements, color, taste and cosmic interrelationships. (Here see the authors' *The Pulse in Occident and Orient*, pp. 125, 121–24, for the flow of energy from organ to organ within twenty-four hours.) The Chinese accommodated to chronobiology as well as to geomagnetic biology with their acupuncture philosophy and techniques.

In these colors is found nature's way to heal and to cure disease. Today Einstein's formula ($E = MC^2$) is applied to the order in the universe. Perhaps if the medical men accepted the view of that which the Hindu philosophy asserts and also implies: namely, that MATTER IS COSMIC COLOR, then medicine would have a philosophy and an empirical basis for the healing power of each individual color.

The Hindus have further devised a table which is useful in prism and color diagnosis. Table 4 below shows the relationship existing among the elements, the sense-organs, the senses and the cosmic colors:[14]

Table 4

ELEMENT	PRINCIPAL RUDIMENT	SENSE ORGAN	COSMIC COLOR
Akasa, Ether	Sound	Ears	Blue
Air	Touch	Skin	Violet
Fire	Form, Sight	Eyes	Red
Water	Taste	Tongue	Orange
Earth	Smell	Nose	Green

12. The **Puranas** aim at incorporating everything in their text. They teach, in addition to the evolutionary theory, that each generating principle or element envelopes the one generated by it. The gross elements combine into a compact mass, the **Brahmanda,** which rests on the waters and is surrounded by seven envelopes—water, wind, fire, air, and three others. Without entering into the chronology of the **Puranas,** one merely notes that the **Kurma** falls into a transitional stage and it accounts for the creation and for the **avataras** of the Vishnu in a summary manner, but mostly in the words employed in the **Vishnu Purana** where the only god Janardana takes the designation of Brahma, Vishnu, and Siva, according as he creates, preserves, or destroys. This is the invariable doctrine of the **Purana,** the only difference being in styling the creator in accordance with the sectarian zeal.

13. Dr. Bhattacharyya uses the reverse form of ROYGBIV to spell VIBGYOR. The author has inserted in the list given above by Dr. Bhattacharyya four other columns: tastes, gems, elements, and polarity. This table capsules Indian medicine. But there is one further explanation: the onyx and the cat's eye as gems are worn or imbibed (in ash-form) to ward off evils of excessive radiation.

14. Dr. B. Bhattacharyya, **The Science of Cosmic Ray Therapy,** Baroda, (India), 1957, p. 30.

If these sense-organs are examined with a prism, the cosmic colors are the same for each organ whether man or beast anywhere in the world. These colors leave the organism at the time of death: for example, the green leaves the tip of the nose at death when the sense of smell is lost.

According to Dr. Bhattacharyya, Ex-Director of the Oriental Institute, the prism is the most effective means of diagnosing by color. To him the color prominent on the face is the offending color which has caused the illness and must be counteracted by the use of the complementary color. He uses a photograph for diagnosis and healing. The reader will find most interesting his exact report of an experience in India:

"A gentleman of about 35 years of age became suddenly ill with very high temperature and delirium at a place 25 miles away, and when news reached here all became anxious. At that moment the photograph of the patient was examined with the prism. The photograph, especially on the face, showed a boiling cauldron in which the colors deep red, deep violet and deep blue were literally boiling, obliterating the face and the sense organs and covering them with a color that was almost black. Under the prism, the eyes, lips, nose, and even the whole face was (sic) covered with dark color and the sense organs could not be distinguished, although next moment when the photograph was seen with the ordinary eyes, it was as bright as ever without any abnormality. It was then proposed to place the photograph on the board in front of the motor fitted with an Emerald disc, and the second copy on the table for prism examination to see whether any change takes place under the action of the Green rays sent out by the motor. As the motor whirled, in a minute or two the black color started fading out, one after another the sense organs such as the eyes, the mouth, the nose became visible, and a beautiful green color pervaded the whole face which started becoming brighter every minute. That afternoon news was received that temperature came down to a bare hundred from 106 degrees, and in three days the patient was well up (sic) again. Under the prism it never showed black color ever afterwards."[15]

India: Clairvoyants

The clairvoyants see these colors associated with the following parts of the body; and in treatment, one should use the complementary colors: e.g., the complementary color for the bone, which is seen by the clairvoyant as green, is red and red should be used. The Indians were among the first to accept the clairvoyant's reports as authentic.

Braincentres-higher-yellow-
   violet
Bone-green
Cerebro-Spinal system-yellow
Circulatory system-blue
Glandular system-violet
Heart-orange
Kidney-indigo

Lungs-yellow
Muscular system-red
Skin-indigo
Sympathetic system with
   heart-orange
Sympathetic system as a
   whole-sea green

India: The Five Elements, the Three Doshas, and the Three Gunas

In the works of Ayurveda is found an explanation of the relationship between the elements in nature and the principles of the

15. This feat is a curious reversal of Oscar Wilde's **The Picture of Dorian Gray.** But there is no room for speculation here. Bardon's explanation furnishes another slant "When taking photographs of the mental plane with all its Elementaries, Elementals, Phantoms and other entities of this sphere, you always need blue filters. For all other beings, deceased people and so forth, violet filters have to be used. And other beings consisting of one element only, such as the essence of the elements, will require ruby red filters, photos of phenomena occurring in nature, mainly concerning the magic of nature, are taken with yellow filters only. As far as the colors are concerned the filters are, therefore, analogous to the respective planes. (Franz Bardon, **Initiation into Hermetics,** Osiris-Verlag, Ketting Uber Koblenz, Western Germany, 1962).

human body. There the three Doshas refer to the five elements: Akasa or Ether, Air, Fire, Water, and Earth.

These three Doshas are distributed among the five great elements constituting the cosmos:

1. The first Dosha—Vayu or harmony—is composed of Akasa and Air.
2. The second Dosha—Pitta or energy—is composed of Fire.
3. The third Dosha—Kapha or inertia—is composed of Water and Earth.

Harmony, energy, and inertia are a three-fold force which contains primordial matter and is inherent in every living cell. These three attributes are in constant motion: uniting, separating, and uniting again, giving shape and form to all living things. Thus the three Doshas correspond to the three Gunas or cosmic attributes. Vayu is conscious manifestation; Pitta is energy; Kapha is resistance or inertia. Whenever Pitta is retarded, it is the result of Kapha. When Pitta decreases, Kapha increases and the reverse is also true. As man grows older, Kapha increases while Pitta decreases, and the harmony of the three attributes is disturbed. This fact accounts for aging. Color can and does restore this equilibrium if applied properly.

India: Mythology

The Hindu pantheon of gods and goddesses presents a bewildering array of names and faculties. For the purposes dictated by this book, only a few figures have been singled out for their relation to color healing on different levels. Very briefly, the Tamil influences (Dravidian Pre-Aryan times) will also be cited as they evolved in the literature of South India. Unlike the Chinese, the Indians have not assigned specific gods to the various organs of the body; color is associated with gods in both cultures, but the Indians are less precise about color than the Chinese. The fetish or sympathetic magic is substituted for organ-god identification in Indian mythology even to this day. An image of a defective arm or eye is presented to the temple: e.g., a golden eye or a golden leg (here is a source of wealth for many of the Indian temples). The notion that the mentally disturbed person is "possessed" prevails in Indian mythology and the choice of a particular deity rests with the individual: e.g., a mentally disturbed woman living near the author has a magician attending her. He plays the drums and chants songs to drive out the spirits (this in the winter of 1964). Custom takes a long time to change especially when the people's belief in magic is associated with healing.

Was Krishna a man or a god? The heroes in mythology are created by the people to answer their particular ideology or needs. Why do the people assess the gods as color equivalents or as electro-magnetic field forces? How are the stories able to describe the positive and negative currents of the person, the race, and the universe? Mythology herein furnishes an evolutionary proof of the unconscious wisdom of the people, the instinct of the self-preservation of the race that is curiously coupled with the instinct of hero-worship: e.g., ennobling Lincoln or Washington. The poet has been termed the unheralded legislator of the future but mythology is the unheralded projection of the wisdom of the eternal human desires told in tales about heroes who once lived, but who were sanctified; told in tales that reveal man's response to the submerged icebergs of the archetypal patterns; told in tales that reflect the wisdom of the race healing itself by devices of which it was or was not conscious.

How is mythology the macroscopic view of man as he follows the race experience and instinct for self-preservation where the senses are not corrupted by civilization and where he must worship a hero? The hero helps man reduce the strain within. This is the innate patterning potential: to get back on the road so man can survive. How is the cell the microscopic view of man as he follows his instinct for self-preservation? When the cell adjusts to a strainer by reverting to its earlier evolutionary pathways, it is using the wisdom of the body which lies embedded in its sub-atomic structural patterning potential. Cell and myth both follow the same patterning potential. When man creates god in his own image, he is ascribing superhuman characteristics to this god. Why?

Among other reasons, to reduce his anxiety and tension. Color does this as the myths reveal. The cell and the myth serve as a unit, one within and the other without: The cell has embedded in itself a feed-back process to utilize the myth for the preservation of the race because the myth is the fundamental basis for the release of abnormal tension and restoration of harmony. The myth is the true sensor-antenna of the environment, and it gives man the right information, puts him on the right frequency. When he loses the pathway, the myth is his compass to direct him back to health.

How is the mind of man relating itself unconsciously or consciously to the archetypal patterns by color and healing? Krishna is useful for an analysis of this interplay. But he must first be projected against the Hindu **Triad of Gods: Brahma, Vishnu, and Siva,**[16] the three deities worshipped all over India. Brahma signified the creator; Siva, the destroyer, and Vishnu, the preserver. Brahma is red, the color of blood and the element of fire; he is the creator even as heat in the body is responsible for creation. Vishnu is blue and signifies air which in space is of a light blue color. Vishnu preserves the world as air preserves life. Siva as Maheswara with his white color is the element of water or phlegm which is white—the destroyer of the world as cold kills by destroying heat.

Krishna

The Krishna problem is one of the most interesting, important, fascinating, and elusive topics in the domain of Indian litera-

---

16. In Indian medicine, the Tridosha represents the extension of the Hindu triad of gods. The theory of Tridosha concerns itself with internal and external conditions, with the production or the loss of equilibrium of the three elements in the human body. With Tridosha, man is not merely a mass of bones, flesh, skin, and chemicals, but a living organism with all parts of the body vibrating with life. Tridosha embraces the whole man and the environs and is an all-embracing theory. Some books state that Tridosha is the crown of the Indian medical science. Nothing can transcend the three elements which permeate the whole world and all names and forms must be traced to their basic elements before they can be of any use to the physician.

ture, but to the orthodox Hindu, Krishna is a reality, and His name has been the saviour of innumerable distressed souls during the last two thousand years. An ordinary Hindu is never concerned with the historicity of Krishna: to investigate the problem is a sacrilege. But scholars have begun to doubt the historicity of Krishna and to maintain that he represents a syncretism of more than one person.

Was Krishna a human being or a divinity at the beginning? Conflicting evidence here supports both the human and divine character of Krishna. Sculptural pieces show that he attained divinity since the third century B.C. Sifting the evidence reveals that Krishna may have been a Vedic seer, a human personality; in the **Mahabharata** is found evidence of the different stages of his deification from the human elements and the human hero to the semi-divine being to the Supreme God. The **Puranas** also show the stages in the deification of the human hero. But some scholars believe that the Krishna of the **Puranas,** the Krishna of the **Mahabharata** and the Krishna of the **Bhagavadgita** are different persons. For purposes of this study, one may say that these irreconcilable features are the property of different cycles of legends. Here the concern is with his significance as a god and his color.

Krishna in human form had a blue skin, was a prince of the Dwarakas and a charioteer to Arjuna. He is also regarded as the incarnation of Vishnu, a paradox explained by the theory of avatars. Allied with the question of his identification with Vishnu is his identification with the god Narayana. But Vishnu is the great benefactor of mankind, the preserver of Dharma or duty and thus Krishna was the follower of Vishnu in preference to malevolent Siva. Vishnu is also a solar deity.

a) The earliest mention of Krishna is of the scholar: a Rishi of that name was a son of Viwaka. There was also a great Asura (so-named) who was defeated and skinned by Indra.
b) In one Vedic hymn, 50,000 Krishnas were said to have been slain, and it is added in another that his pregnant wives were slain with him so that he could leave no posterity. This is sup-

posed to have reference to the Rakshasas or to the dark-colored aborigines of India.

c) Krishna—a handsome cowherd and cattle tender—wooed and won the hearts of many young ladies, married and unmarried.

d) The modern deity Krishna is the most celebrated hero of Indian mythology and the most popular of all the deities. He appears prominently in the **Mahabharata** where his character is invested with a certain degree of mysticism. Additions and interpolations have raised him to divinity, and it is in the character of the "Divine One" that he delivered the celebrated song **Bhagavad-Gita** now held to be a part of the great epic.

e) Krishna is a solar deity.

Different Interpretations of Krishna's Blue Color and His Role in Healing: Forty-Nine as a Mystical Number

Different accounts of Tamil literature use the number forty-nine in a mystical way. One Academy is said to have lived in 4449 and another account lists 549 poets. Forty-nine here is a vibration significant in color healing. Why?

> Man lives on the forty-ninth color vibration.
> Blue used on the forty-ninth vibration heals.
> Blue used beyond the forty-ninth vibration destroys.

The **Puranas,** as mentioned in an early footnote, explain how **Brahmanda** which rests on the waters is surrounded by seven envelopes—water, wind, fire, air, ahamkara (arrogance that destoys man), buddhi (intelligence that may or may not become wisdom), and pradhana. In the **Brahmanda,** the highest deity which is invested with the guna activity appeared in the form of Brahma and created all things. The same deity in the **guna sattva** preserves, as Vishnu, the universe until the end of a Kalpa, or an eon of time, when the same god in the awful form of Rudra destroys it. Then is described the raising of the earth from beneath the waters by Narayana in the form of a boar, and the creation of earth, sky, heaven and **Maharloka** (sea and world of fish).

In South India to this day, the name of the god Narayana is chanted to ward off evil. And Narayana is another name for the gods Vishnu and Krishna, all of them being associated with the color blue. **Blue can heal or destroy!** At present man's life is confined by the limits posed by his position on the forty-ninth vibration. Once it passes out of the particular range of conditions, it is destroyed. These three ideas: destruction, preservation and limitation by nature of species—are reflected in their mythology.

In Indian thought, modern man is living in the Kali age, but this term Kali is pronounced differently from the goddess Kali, who is associated with destruction. Kali of time, signifies evil. This is the age of Kali evil when all life will be destroyed. The color of black is associated with Kali. Krishna may be blue-black. The Kalp-Rudra-Narayana story of the **Puranas** means the destruction of one age and the rise of another age. Is this another stage in the evolutionary spiral? Is man moving into another vibration out of the forty-ninth? Is man going to a more spiritual level? In scientific terms, is man going from a denser mass to a less dense mass? If there is less density in man, he would have greater mobility in space. The colors blue-black associated with Krishna and Narayana have always been both healing and destructive.

Krishna's Blue and Reich's Blue Orgone: Is There a Relationship? In the **Rigveda,** three words are of consequence to this study of color: **Krishna, Drapsa,** and **Amsumati** because they have been variously interpreted.

Krishna and Drapsa

1. Refers to soma, said one scholar.
2. Means the swift moving Krishna, an Asura who with 10,000 occupied the banks of the Amsumati or Yamuna.
3. Are two identical and not two inimical forces.
4. Is the sperm of Brahaspathi, hidden in the river.
5. Is Soma as attacked by Krishna and saved by Indra.
6. Is the darkened moon, and Amsumati is a mystical river of the air in which the moon dips to recover its vanished light, and 10,000 are probably demons of darkness.

In these interpretations are found all the characteristics of Reich's orgone theory and cosmic super-imposition and sex: the dipping of the moon in the blue orgone ocean, etc.

c) Krishna the Flutist.

Krishna was a superb musician; this vibration is related to color and light, and healing. After the review of the Hindu triad and the study of Krishna, attention must be devoted to Sakti.

Sakti—(Durga, Kali, Chandi, and Bhairavi)

The "Goddess" or Maha-devi, wife of the gos Siva and daughter of Himavat or the Himalayan mountains. As the Sakti or female energy of Siva, she has two characters: one mild, the other fierce; and it is under the latter that she is especially worshipped. She has a great variety of names, referable to her various forms, attributes, actions, but these names are not always used accurately and distinctively. As

1. Uma, she is "Light" and represents a type of beauty;
2. Gauri, she is "the yellow or Brilliant";
3. Parvathi, the mountaineer and
4. Himavathi—from her parentage;
5. Jagan-mata, she is the "mother of the world."
   In her terrible forms, she is worshipped as
6. Durga, "the inaccessible";
7. and 8. Kali and Syama—"the black";
9. Chandi and Chandika—"the fierce";
10. Bhairavi—"the terrible." It is in this character that bloody sacrifices are offered to her, that the barbarities of the Durga-puja and the Charak-Puja are perpetrated in her honor, and that the orgies of the Tantrikas are held to propitiate her favours and celebrate her powers. She has ten arms, and in most of her hands, there are weapons. As Durga, she is a beautiful yellow woman riding on a tiger in a fierce and menacing attitude.

As Kali or Kalika, "the black", she is represented with a black skin, a hideous and terrible countenance, dripping with blood, encircled with snakes, hung round with skulls and human heads, and in all respects resembling a fury rather than a goddess.

As Vindhya-vasini, "the dweller in the Vindhyas", she is worshipped at a place of that name where the Vindhyas approach the Ganges, near Mirzapur, and it is said that there the blood before her image is never allowed to get dry. As Mahamaya she is the great illusion.

The Durga-Puja is a human sacrifice that exists to this day in India. The Howrah Bridge, in Calcutta (a city dedicated to the goddess Kali), was built, so folk tradition repeats, with a child sacrificed for each arch constructed. Another example was repeated as a story told to the author about a college in Madurai, a town in South India famous for its temple. Seven carpenters were killed in a train accident on their way to work on the college building. Their death led the natives to comment. "The building is now on a firm foundation. The blood sacrifice has been made." In India today, specially fattened goats or cocks are sacrificed to Kali. One odd fact that was reported to the author by his servant who had eaten the sacrificial flesh: the food was tasteless. Whenever a building is constructed or when a field has yielded a good crop, a straw effigy is erected to ward off the "evil eye."

Savitr in the **Rig veda,** is stimulator, a form of the Sun God personifying the divine power of the sun. He alone is the lord of vivifying power, the exciter of all motion and activity. The Golden handed Savitr moves between heaven and earth; he sets the sun in motion. He is a divine physician who drives away disease (removes it); he bestows long life on man. In modern science, he would represent heliotherapy.

Varuna is one of the oldest deities of the Vedas, where he ranks only second to Indra and in many respects his position is comparable with that of Zeus in the Green pantheon. He is also closely related, at least in function, to the Iranian Ahura Mazada. As lord over all, he is closely associated with Mitra, a sun god, and is a healing seer.

In Tamil folk lore, Varuna is a rain god and Indra, as god of the clouds, has the cloud for his vehicle. The Varuna-Indra myth may be interpreted as the basic element water, vital to life. In times of drought, the Indian kings would perform a yaga or sacrificial fire which would be made with ghee or oil poured on the flames so that the smoke ascending to the heavens would please the gods who would then bless the earth with rain.

Kaman is the Indian god of love who sends his arrows of flowers into the breasts of his victims to create turmoil. The five flowers which Kaman uses in his sugar-cane bow are the lotus (white or red); the Mango (yellow-orange); the Asoka (white); the wild jasmine (white and very fragrant); and the blue water lily. One day he threw an arrow at Siva who became annoyed so that he sent out a ray of fire from his central or third eye. This spark burned Kaman's body so that he lost his form. But his wife Rathi begged Siva to restore her husband's form. So Siva decreed that only to his wife would Kaman assume form. To all others, he would be formless.

The fire from the centre of Siva's forehead is really the pituitary gland which controls all the glands of the body. It is used in healing and in **Nu Reflex Therapy** (by the author) as one of the key points. In mythology, the third eye is a sign of spirituality, knowledge, and a high degree of development. Thus the Siva spark of energy is destructive or constructive.

Buddha—See China

The Green Gooseberry legend in Tamil mythology has certain resemblances to the Chinese myth recounting longevity. A certain gooseberry tree, not a bush, blossomed once in every hundred years and bore only one green berry. Whoever ate of this fruit would live a very long time. The king Athihaman, in admiration for the talents of the poetess Av-vai, gave her the rare gooseberry and with it, the gift of long life.

Agasthiar is here included though history reports thirty-seven men of this name who have made contributions to healing.

He was known as a great Tamil scholar, a healer who advocated the use of a wise diet and living according to natural laws. He taught and used color and sound in the healing of the sick in South India. This is of consequence since the Tamil language is an early Dravidian tongue which preceded Sanskrit and has least the Sanskrit influence.

China: Contribution to Color Healing

The Chinese doctor uses many different techniques:

1. Looking or observation;
2. Hearing;
3. Questioning;
4. Feeling or a palpation. His complete examination includes consideration as well of the following but the reader is warned that the author does not attempt to include the seven emotions, the twelve official systems and the twelve anatomical charts.
5. The Five Colors: Green, Yellow, Red, White and Black.
6. The Five Elements: Metal, Wood, Earth, Water, Fire.
7. The Five Tastes: Salt, Sweet, Sour, Bitter and Pungent.
8. The Four Situations: East, South, West and North.
9. The Four Seasons[17] are utilized in the following:

Spring: Green color; Element is Wood; Situation is East; pertains to the liver.

Summer: Red Color; Element is Fire; Situation is South; pertains to the Heart.

Autumn: White color; Element is Metal; Situation is West; pertains to the Lungs.

Winter: Orange color; Element is Water; Situation is North; pertains to the Kidneys.

17. This principle is used in radio. Best reception is received when antennae face in the direction of the signal. Among the Mexican Indians, pains are called serpents and are of four colors in order to relate them to the cardinal points. There are the Blue, Yellow, Red, and White serpents.

How does the Chinese doctor apply these principles to the ailing man? Obviously this book can provide only a random sampling of the application. All the organs are considered as having a certain relationship with corresponding organs. The large intestines to the lungs, the spleen to the stomach, the bladder to the kidney and the gall bladder to the liver etc.

The stomach color is yellow (see 5 above); its element is earth (See 6 above); the situation is South (See 8 above); and the total man is interpreted in the light of the season. (See Chinese Astrology). The same can be worked out for any other organ.

China: Astrology

Astrology can be said to be the left hand of the Chinese physician and is used in diagnosis: for example, if a person is born under the sign of Leo, his nature is warm, his complexion is dark red, and he cannot bear long exposure to the sun nor digest stimulating foods. Chinese astrology was developed by the Chinese themselves and is considered an old science tested by time and used in daily living. Astrology has been known by every people, but the Chinese as well as the Indians use it as an anatomical instrument linked up with the five planets which correspond to the five elements, and applied to the human body (See table below). In physiology, it signifies food values and is used as a science of nutrition.

Table 5

Planets	Five Elements	Organs	Colors	Physiognomy
Venus	Metal	Lungs	White	Stout
Jupiter	Wood	Liver	Green	Slim
Mercury	Water	Kidney	Orange	Fat
Mars	Fire	Heart	Red	Thin
Saturn	Earth	Stomach	Yellow	Stocky

China: Auras

The auras in Chinese culture are usually written as an ideogram on the sands. The spirit is formally invited to attend, and the medium is protected during the ceremony. When the spirit leaves, the ideogram in the sand is then translated. Not much stress was laid on the auras in Chinese thought. They developed a theory of Yin and Yang which satisfied them. In general, the Indians try to influence the aura by thought and by meditation on the mental plane and by exercises in Hatha Yoga on the physical. The Chinese, being more pragmatic and perhaps less imaginative, did not trouble with the individual auras. They developed a system of healing, called Acupuncture, that influences the electro-magnetic forces. Unlike the Hindus who use meditation and concentration, the Chinese devised a system where the physician did it for them.

China: Yin and Yang (Animus and Anima) Death, the Golden Light

The Hindus use the term prahna to mean a vital energy in man that is cosmic energy, an indestructible force. On death, prahna leaves the body. There is no such equivalent in Chinese Taoism or Buddhism, but an attempt will be made to explain certain aspects bearing on the search for and the belief in the indestructible: in the Golden Light.

Throughout life, man has two opposing, but not antagonistic forces: the Yang and the Yin. Yang is positive and masculine and Yin is negative and feminine. They both move in cycles and constantly change in their relationship to themselves and to each other. (Wilhelm and Jung have called the Yang the Animus and the Yin the Anima to conform to their psychological outlook). The Chinese Hexagrams in the **I Ching** reveal these changing relationships between the Yin and the Yang forces and the consequent ebb and flow, flux and change of the life forces that constitute vitality. Thus, the end goal of awareness to the followers is to walk in the golden light. At death, Yin (or Anima) sinks to earth and Yang (or Animus) is free to walk into the great golden light which is a new vibration.

This analogy may be used: Suppose a circle of men and women were talking in a room when an atom bomb destroyed everyone sitting there. Those trained in cultivating their bodies to walk in the light, would leave their physical bodies on the floor and would become a flood light of bright color and vibration so that they could continue talking on their other level. The quest in meditation and concentration is no quest: just a letting go into the void or being in the void of the Golden Light or becoming the Golden Flower.[18]

Warner's **A Dictionary of Chinese Mythology** defines Yin and Yang in the following fashion:

The negative and positive principles of universal life. These words mean originally the dark and bright sides of a sunlit bank, and occur on the Stone Drums (eighth century B.C.). By the time of Confucius, they had acquired a philosophical significance as two aspects of the duality which Chinese thinkers perceived in all things. Traces of the dual notion occur in the "Great Plan" of the **Shu ching,** but the actual words Yin and Yang as used in this sense first occur in the pseudo-Confucian commentaries on the **I Ching.**

In this way, Yang came to mean Heaven, Light, Vigour, Male, Penetration, The Monad. It is symbolized by the Dragon and is associated with azure color and oddness in numbers. In Fengshui, raised land forms (mountains) are Yang.

Similarly Yin stands for earth (the antithesis of heaven), Darkness, Quiescence, Female, Absorption, The Duad. It is symbolized by the Tiger and is associated with orange color and even numbers. Valleys and streams possess the Yin Quality.

---

18. See R. Wilhelm (Translated and Explained by) **The Secret of the Golden Flower, a Chinese Book of Life, with a European Commentary by C.G. Jung,** Wehman Bros., Broadway, N.Y., 3, N.Y., 1955, pp. 12-19; (translated into English by C.F. Baynes).

The two are represented by a whole and a broken line respectively, thus: —Yang --Yin

Groups of three such lines are known as "trigrams," groups of six as "Hexagrams," and the **I Ching** is classified under the sixty-four possible hexagrams.

In connection with the five elements (or natural forces), the Yin and Yang have been for at least two thousand years used to interpret the processes of nature and they are the fundamental feature in the theories which underlie Feng-shui, Astrology, Divination, and medicine.

The Yin and Yang principles have been deified as Tung Wang-Kung, the Royal Mother of the West. The Royal father lives in a kind of paradise in the Eastern Ocean. The Royal Mother rules in the Kung-Lun Mountains, which are said to be the junction point between Heaven and Earth, and the place where the Yin and the Yang vapours are harmonized. Once each year, Hsi Wang-mu goes to her husband, crossing over the back of Yin and Yang a gigantic bird which is said to overshadow them, and they spend a short space of time in each other's company. This bird is known as the "rare bird".

T'ak Yang means the Sun; T'ai Yin, the moon; Shao Yang, the fixed stars, and Shao Yin, the planets. These four beings are supposed to be the four primary combinations of Yin and Yang.

But Yin and Yang are themselves supposed to have proceeded from a "great Ultimate," **T'ai Chi.**

China: Mythology—Hsi Wang-Mu was the Western Royal Mother; she was also paired with **Mu King.** This deity was formed of the pure quintessence of the Western Air. As **Mu King,** formed of Eastern Air, he is the active Yang principle of the male air and sovereign of the Eastern Air; so **Hsi Wang-Mu,** born of the Western air, is the passive or female Yin principle and sovereign of the Western Air. These two principles, co-operating, engender Heaven and Earth and all the beings of the universe, and thus become the two principles of life and of the subsistence of all that exists. She is the head of the troop of genii dwelling on the K'un-lun Mountains (the Taoist equivalent of the Buddhist Sumeru), and from time to time holds intercourse with favoured imperial votaries.

Hsi Wang-Mu's palace is situated in the high mountains of the snowy K'un-lun. It is 1000 li (about 333 miles) in circuit; a rampart of massive gold surrounds its battlements of precious stones. Its right wing rises on the edge of Ts'ui Ho, the Jasper River. It is the usual abode of the immortals, who are divided into seven special categories according to the color of their garments—red, blue, black, violet, yellow, green, and "nature-color." There is a marvellous fountain built of precious stones, where the periodical banquet of the immortals is held. This feast is called P'an-t-ao Hui the Feast of Peaches.

It takes place on the borders of Jasper Lake and is attended by both male and female Immortals. Besides several superfine meats, they are served with bears' paws, monkeys' lips, dragons' liver, phoenix' marrow, and peaches gathered in the orchard, endowed with the mystic virtue of conferring longevity on all who have the good luck to taste them. It required three thousand years for the fruit to ripen. These were Hsi Wang-Mu's birthdays, when all the Immortals assembled for the great feast, "...the occasion being more festive than solemn for there was music on invisible instruments, and songs not from mortal tongues." From the ceremony arose the custom of presenting women of fifty and over the image of Hsi Wang-Mu.

Chun T'I The Goddess of the Dawn or the Goddess of Light. As Maritchi, she was represented as a female with eight arms, two of which held aloft the sun and the moon. She was the protectress against war. With the Hindus, Taoists, and Japanese Buddhists, she is a stellar divinity, residing in the Great Bear. When the goddess is represented with three heads, the one on the right is that of a sow (in China and Japan, on the right; in India on the left). Having appropriated her from Buddhism, the Taoists set her up in their own pantheon, in the seventh and eighth centuries A.D. She then was no longer the Goddess of the Dawn, but an Immortal with warlike attributes (like Kali-Uma). Tantra Buddhism represented her as a warlike being with sixteen or eighteen arms. Nowadays she is worshipped both in Buddhist and Taoists temples. "The original idea is almost entirely ignored, except in pictorial art. . ."

Chung K'uei:

The Emperor Ming Huang (A.D. 713-56) when attacked by a fever dreamt that he saw a small demon fantastically dressed in red trousers, with a shoe on one foot—but none on the other, and a shoe hanging from his girdle. The emperor questioned him and asked his name. He replied his name was Emptiness and Devastation. Suddenly a great devil appeared, wearing a tattered head-covering and blue robe, a horn clasp on his belt, and official boots on this feet. He went up to the spirit, tore out one of his eyes, crushed it up, and ate it.

The Emperor then asked the newcomer who he was. "Your humbler servant," he replied, "is Chung K'uei, Physician of Chung nan Shan in Shensi. In the reign of Emperor Kao Tsu (A.D. 618-27), I was ignominiously rejected and unjustly defrauded of a first class in the public examinations. Overwhelmed with shame, I committed suicide on the steps of the imperial Palace. The Emperor ordered me to be buried in a green robe (reserved for members of the imperial clan), and out of gratitude for that favour, I swore to protect the sovereign in any part of the Empire against the evil of the demon Hus Hao." At these words, the Emperor awoke and found that the fever had left him.

Chung K'uei, his name, is used to frighten away evil spirits. The demon signifies fever; the devil in blue reduces fever; the Emperor wakes up cured of his fever. A perfect example of color therapy!

Gods of the Kidneys and the Liver

The God of the Left Kidney was Ch'un Yuan-chen, his body being three and seven-tenths inches in height and his color varying: white, red, green, or any of the five colors.

The God of the Right Kidney was Hsiang Ti-wu; his designation Tao Sheng; his body three and a half inches in height; his color white or black.

The God of the Liver had two names: K'aui-chun; six inches; color yellowish blue; Fang Ch'ang, Style or Measure, Tzu Yuan.

Buddha is interpreted as possessing thirty-two principles of beauty, and most prominent is his golden yellow color. Chiefly to be stressed for application to modern healing practices are these:

a) He possessed a perfect spine. This is the basis for chiropractic and physical medicine.

b) He had very long ear lobes. In Yoga and in Nu Reflex Therapy, the ear lobes play a very important part in regeneration and healing.

c) In Samadhi and at death, his figure is depicted with one leg longer than the other. In Nu Reflex Therapy, this difference in leg length is a method used both in diagnosis and in healing.

d) Each hair of his head curls to the right, one hair for each pore, in a right handed turn. This confirms Sir William Lawrence Bragg's statement that man is nothing but a "right handed cork screw." The application of this principle to modern biochemistry is very important. The Galvihara stone figure of the reclining Buddha seen at Polonnaruwa, Ceylon signally reveals these qualities.

Part II

How to Heal with Color

CHAPTER III

HOW TO LOSE OR GAIN WEIGHT WITH COLOR

The reader is being directly introduced to healing by color, for he is here given a set of directives that he can follow and test by his personal body responses and his individual needs. If he is in need of losing weight, let him read the directions that follow to understand how to apply color therapy to his individual needs. If he wishes to gain weight, let him study the outlined directives that apply to his particular need. Self-interest and self-motivation will quickly teach him how readily to comprehend one of the purposes of this study.

This remedial use of color works. The practice is based on sound scientific principles that have met with much success throughout the world. These principles further act in conformity with natural laws which are timeless, universal, and immutable. Simply phrased, one may add that color therapy is a natural and rational means of preventive and remedial medicine.

General Introduction to Diet

The most popular topic in periodicals today is diet. There is the high protein diet and the high carbohydrate diet; there is the low protein diet and the low carbohydrate diet. Some individuals count their calories as if they were counting money and others do not care. Some swear by the Schmendrick diet, and others swear at it. Some people eat like horses and remain thin; others eat like horses and look like them. The vegetarian is certain that meat is the cause of all human ailments, and the carnivorous individual sneers at "rabbit food." One expert claims Food A is the wonder food; another claims Food B is; and a third states Foods A and B are bad for man. Maybe all are right—like the judge who heard a husband testify against his wife. He complained that she was bad, and the judge nodded his head and remarked, "You are right." When the wife testified about her husband, the judge, replying to her complaints, said, "You are right." When the judge's wife then reminded her husband that they both could not be right, his reply to her was. "You too, are right, my dear."

A large part of the population starves for months to lose weight and then in a matter of days puts it all back; they go from Schmendrick diet to the Nebich diet, to whatever diet is popular at that particular time. But their weight remains the same. Then another large part seeks to gain weight. They eat foods rich in calories and do not worry about cholesterol, but they still wear size thirteen collars. Diet is like the Mexican lottery; only instead of having half the population selling tickets and the other half buying them, one half the population is trying to lose weight and the other half trying to gain.

One doctor says it is the thyroid at fault; another, the liver or the pituitary. The Patients need Vitamin X; they need Vitamin Y; they need a new approach to living. Both the overweight and the underweight individuals are suffering from the same disease: an imbalance in the body and an imbalance of color. Why color? Because food is nothing more than color materialized by the plant. The plant takes the light and makes food by the process of photosynthesis. When man digests the food, he breaks down the material form back into light and color. Light is the connecting link between consciousness and pattern, between idea and form, and in the growing plant is seen a direct relationship between light and the emergence of pattern.

Thinness or underweight is the result of an imbalance between blue and red rays. If one is underweight, the condition is the result of an overdose of red rays or a shortage or lack of blue rays. To restore balance, the body must be exposed to blue rays, must eat foods containing the blue rays of the spectrum, and must sip solarized blue water twice daily.

Overweight is due to an imbalance in the body between the red and the blue rays of the spectrum. Corpulence is the result of an overdose of blue rays or the lack of red rays in the body. To restore balance and harmony, the body must be exposed to red rays, must eat food containing the red rays, and must sip solarized red-ray water twice daily.

Losing Weight with Color

Overweight is the result of an imbalance between the red and blue rays that the body extracts mainly from foods and from other sources. The individual who is overweight and who wishes to lose weight will work on this principle:

> The body suffers from an insufficiency of red rays because it has an overabundance of blue rays. The body is overdosed with blue rays and underdosed with red rays.

How to add red rays to the body? How to tune in, vibrate with, and absorb the needed red rays? Follow the steps indicated below with this precaution: Never increase the time limits for exposure to light. If in doubt, underexpose. **Never Overexpose.** Infra-red rays should **never** be used.

Four Steps to Build a Reserve of Red Rays

I. Expose the Body to a Bath of Red Light.

1) Assemble your equipment: a lamp with a red bulb, at least fifteen watts (here the **Exit** bulb, so labeled because of its use and amounting to seventy five watts, is readily available); a second lamp with a regulation white light, frosted or unfrosted; a clock-timer; a set of records: fast-moving tempo, exciting, or martial music that arouses one to action or stimulates one. Arrange records on recorder for thirty or forty minutes of uninterrupted music.

2) Arrange your equipment in such a way about your bed or about wherever you choose to stretch out or to sit that without too much movement of your body and without disturbing your relaxed position you can turn on your lights, adjust your timer, and listen to the music. Assure yourself of complete privacy.

3) Start your recorder and then lie down on your bed and relax your nude body; attempt to remove irritating or annoying thoughts from your mind. Give yourself about two minutes to be stimulated by the challenging recorded music.

4) Adjust your timer to a five minute warning signal; then turn on the white light and allow the white light to shine on your head and body while you listen to the stirring music.

5) When the five minute warning signal sounds, readjust your timer to ring in ten minutes; then turn off the white light and turn on the red light.

   Allow the red light to shine on your head and body, especially your stomach, your back, and your feet. Let the red rays flood the body. Make sure the bulb does not burn you.

6) When the ten minute signal is sounded, turn off the red light immediately.

7) Then turn on the white light and adjust your timer to a fifteen minute warning termination. Allow the white light to shine on your head and body while your stimulated self continues to listen to the exciting music.

Caution:

   If the individual using red for some time should feel feverish and exhausted, he should switch to an orange bulb. If he has a definite fever or diarrhea that lasts for more than one day, he should switch to a blue light for five minutes—not for ten—and follow with fifteen minutes of white light. The day after the condition abates, he should return to use of red light.

   Individuals who have hypertension or tachycardia should substitute an orange bulb for a red bulb. Red will raise the blood pressure which is contra-indicated in the cases of hypertension or tachycardia whereas orange will stimulate and raise the pulse rate without raising the blood pressure.

8) This procedure of music and exposure to two different light rays must be followed for at least forty five days, but need not be followed for more than sixty days. . . . **Possibly without any interruption in the daily routine so that a patterned behaviour-response to this red color is established.** Remember the goal: To restore proper balance

of red rays to the body. It would be effective to expose the body at the same time everyday. The best moments for charging the body with these energizing rays are sunrise, sunset, and the median hour of noon, but the individual is merely advised to choose a half hour of time which could be regularly followed as far as his program permits. Firm adherence to the hour and the moment is recommended, but is not inflexibly insisted upon. Let the individual use his common sense in following out a reasonably consistent program with some type of regularity.

What is stressed is the matter of daily exposure: These interstellar light charges irradiate the body batteries; hence these daily cosmic charges are imperative. Remember: Daily Cosmic Charges!

Think what happens to your car battery if your charger fails to function. Within a day, your car is immobilized. The body must adapt to the new patterns; hence regularity is stressed.

II. Eat Foods Rich with the Red Rays of spectrum.

The person who seeks to lose weight should select foods rich with the red rays of the spectrum; that means the foods must be liberally endowed with red, yellow, orange rays. The following list will partially and briefly enumerate these foods:

RED	YELLOW	ORANGE
Beets	Apricots	All Orange-Skinned
Cabbage	Butter	Fruits and Vegetables
Cherries	Carrots	Carrots
Egg-Plant	Cantalope	Pumpkins
Meat	Corn	Rutabaga
Onion	Grapefruit	
Pepper	Lemon	
Radishes	Mangoes	
Red-Skinned	Melon	
Fruits and	Orange	
Vegetables	Onion	

RED	YELLOW
Strawberries	Papaya
Tomatoes	Peach
Watercress	Persimmon
Watermelon	Squash
Yams	Tangerine
	Turnip
	Yolk of egg

III. Drink Red-Solarized Water.

What is red-solarized water? It is water in a red container that has been exposed to and irradiated by the rays of the sun.

How can it be prepared? Select a red glass, a red bottle, or any glass container, ruby-red in color. Fill it up with water and place the container where the sun will shine directly upon both container and its contents. Expose this bottle for at least one hour so that the sun acting upon the water through the red glass will charge the water with its red rays.

If glass of the requisite red shade is not available, red filters may be used.

Caution:

The container with red rays should be changed every two days in hot weather and every 10 days in the winter. The necessary precaution should be taken in cold weather to see that glass does not freeze and break. Allow for expansion—so do not fill the container to the brim.

IV. Visualize Red and Then Direct use of Color-Breathing through Meditation.

For those trained in meditation and mental suggestion, visualization of color and direct use of color in color-breathing may be used. *Note:* Change in time of treatment is stressed here as being extremely important.

1. Breathe deeply and regularly as prescribed for meditation.

2. Visualize white rays coming into the body from the head and downward; these white rays sweep down and into the body

and envelop the body externally and internally. Do this for **two minutes.**

3. Then visualize red rays as streaming up from the earth, into the soles of the feet and mounting up in waves to the top of the head. Concentrate on this upward waving motion through the feet for **two minutes only.**

4. Then concentrate on white rays (Repeat step 2); for five minutes let cosmic white radiant energy bathe you. Now you function in balance and in harmony between the red and the blue rays.

Gaining Weight with Color

Underweight is the result of an imbalance between the red and the blue rays that the body extracts from food. The individual who is slender and wishes to build up his body by adding weight will work on this principle:

The body suffers from insufficiency of blue rays because it has an overabundance of red rays.
It is overdosed with red rays and underdosed with blue rays.

How will he add blue rays to his body? How will he tune into, vibrate to, and absorb the needed blue rays? Follow the steps indicated below with this warning:

Never increase the time limits indicated. If in doubt, underexpose. **Never Overexpose!**

Four Steps to Build a Reserve of Blue Rays

I. Expose the Body to a Bath of Blue Light.

1. Assemble your equipment: a lamp with a blue bulb, at least fifteen watts, but it could be more; a lamp with a white light bulb, frosted or unfrosted, such as is used every day; a clock-timer; a set of records of soothing music restfully relaxing and peaceful—arranged, if possible, on a recorder that will play for at least thirty to forty minutes.

2. Place the equipment in such a way about the bed that without disturbing your relaxed position and without too much movement of the body, you can turn on your light, adjust your timer, and listen to your music. Assure yourself of complete privacy.

3. Start your recorder and then lie down on your bed and relax your nude body; attempt to remove irritations and annoyances from your mind. Give yourself about one or two minutes to be relaxed and quiescently attentive to the music.

4. Adjust your timer to a five minute warning signal. Then turn on the white light and allow it to shine on your head and body while you listen to the soft music.

5. When the five minute signal is given, adjust your timer to the ten minute signal; turn off the white light and turn on the blue light. Allow the blue light to shine on your head first and then on your body.

6. When the ten minute warning signal sounds, turn off the blue light immediately.

7. Then turn on the white light and adjust your timer to a fifteen minute warning termination. Allow the white light to shine on your head and body while your relaxed consciousness listens to the music and avoids all annoying thoughts.
    Caution: if the patient has hypertension, a green or light blue bulb instead of indigo should be used.

8. This procedure of music and exposure to two different light rays must be followed for at least forty-five days, but not for more than sixty days: **Possibly without any interruption in the daily routine so that a Patterned behavior-response to the blue color is established.** Remember the goal: Restore proper balance to the body of blue rays.

It would be effective to expose the body at the same time every day. Without stressing the fact that the best moments for charging the body with these energizing rays are sunrise, sunset, and the median hour of noon, the individual is merely advised to choose a half hour of time which could be regularly followed as far as his program permits. Firm adherence to the hour and the moment is recommended, but is not inflexibly insisted upon. Let the individual use his common sense in following out a reasonably consistent program with some type of regularity.

What is stressed is the matter of daily exposure: These interstellar light charges irradiate the body batteries. Hence these daily cosmic charges are imperative. Remember: Daily Cosmic Charges!

Think what happens to your car battery if your charger fails in its duty. Within a day, your car is immobilized. The body must adapt to the new patterns; hence regularity is stressed.

II. Eat Foods Rich with the Blue Rays of the Spectrum.

The slender person who seeks to add to his body weight should select foods rich in the blue rays of the spectrum. The following are some of the basic foods endowed by nature with the requisite blue rays combined with white rays:

All blue-skinned	Pears	Potato
Fruits and	Asparagus	Fish
Vegetables	Celery	Chicken
Blueberries	Parsnip	Veal
Plums		
Grapes		

III. Drink Blue-Solarized Water.

What is blue-solarized water? It is water in a blue container that has been exposed to and irradiated by the sun. How can it be prepared?

Select a blue glass, a blue bottle, or any glass container of color desired: indigo, blue or violet. Fill it three-fourths full of water. Place the container and its contents in the sun or expose this bottle for at least one hour so that the sun acting upon the water through the glass will charge the water with the blue rays.

If glass of the requisite blue shading is not available, blue filters may be used.

Since these blue rays are antiseptic, the water so irradiated may keep for about a week or ten days. Caution must be taken to keep the glass from cracking or the water from freezing in cold weather. That is why the container is only three-fourths filled.

IV. Visualize Blue and Then Direct Use of Color-breathing Through Meditation. For those trained in meditation and mental suggestion, visualization of color and direct use of color breathing may be used. But there is a change in time duration.

1. Breath deeply and regularly, as prescribed for meditation.
2. Visualize white rays streaming into the head from the cosmic atmosphere. Concentrate on this for **two minutes only.**
3. Visualize blue rays streaming into the fontanels (the soft spot on the baby's head; hardened in the adults') and shooting downward in the body. Do this for two minutes only. Try projecting the blue rays from the fontanels to the other part of the body. In that way, body balance will be attained.
4. Then concentrate on white light and let cosmic energy bathe you for five minutes. See yourself as functioning in balance with red and blue rays in harmony.

CHAPTER IV

· PROPERTIES OF COLOR

A. General properties of Color

1. Light possesses atomicity. Color in the form of light is part of the electro-magnetic spectrum.[1]
2. All electro-magnetic waves are identical in wave length and frequency.
3. All types of radiant energy travel at the same rate of speed: 186,000 miles per second, and this figure divided by the wave length of each establishes its frequency.
4. Each color has a definite wave length from 1/16 to 1/32 millionth of an inch and therefore varies in frequency and impact force.
5. The value of each hue is controlled by its amplitude, light values having greater amplitude than dark ones.
6. The waves of the electro-magnetic spectrum serve an almost limitless number of uses: radio, television, infra-red photography, ultra-violet lamps, fluorescent light, X-rays, etc.
7. Variations in the impact on the eye affect muscular, mental and nervous activity. Tests show that under ordinary light, muscular activity is 23 empirical units. It advances slightly under blue light. Green light increases it a little more. Yellow raises it to 30 units. Subject a person to a green color for as much as five minutes, and his mental as well as physical activity changes. The action of color is specialized. Each color reacts to and draws into the body a special current of vital energy from the environment.

---

1. The Doppler effect applies to light and sound waves. Light waves appear to the eye as longer when they come from an object moving away from the observer; they seem shorter and crowded if the object is approaching the observer. With light the effect shows up in color. Light waves are longer at the red end of the spectrum and shorter at the violet end. Light waves coming from an object moving away from the observer shift down the spectrum toward the red end, a pheonomenon called the "Red Shift."

B. Physical and Physiological properties of Color.

8. Color has force, weight, action, and temperature. These are the basic properties of color; all the other properties are extensions and refinements of these four. (This is the key to color healing similar to the use of numbers from zero to nine in mathematics).

9. The temperature of color—heat vs. cold:

Red, orange, yellow and infra-red are heating rays; they produce heat and power to create chemical reactions in the body.

The greater the resistance, the greater the heat. Red combined with yellow has the most penetrating power. Blue, violet, and ultra-violet are cooling rays.

Measurement of heat: There are various amounts of heat in color rays. Measure by placing a thermometer in a colored glass of water; red rays give off the most heat and blue rays the least amount.

10. The force and weight of color: Measure these properties by shining a ray of light on a sensitively balanced scale. The scale will tip in the direction of the light.

11. The action of color—the stepping-up or down of vibrations: all forms of energy or vibration are related and can easily be stepped up or down into another vibration. Heat can be stepped up to light which when applied to the plant, is vital for its nutrition, growth, and reproduction.

C. Inter-Related Properties of Color

Note: From this point on, no attempt is made to show the application of the enumerated principles to other specific principles because they all weave a tapestry of interrelationship.

12. Light vs. dark as a property:

Yellow and green are light rays (the term light does not mean the light end of the spectrum).

Blue, violet, and indigo are the dark rays.

Dark rays do not penetrate as well as the lighter ones and often not through glass. The psychological effects are derived from the light or dark rays.

13. The mixing of pigments does not produce the same color as the mixing of light rays of the spectrum.
14. Disease is manifested as color through energy-equivalents. Every disease causes the body to give off energy. The energy differs as the disease differs. All of these energies have colors.

    The diseased condition in the body can therefore be identified by the color which is given off. **Every disease has a specific vibration which is uniform and invariable.**
15. Every individual has a normal rhythm which is changed by imbalance of body tissue. The rhythm may become too fast or too slow.
16. Do not treat the name of the disease or its vibration alone; treat the individual's total color needs.
17. Between the extremities of the positive and negative poles, there is an endless diversity in rate and vibration.
18. Negative energy or electricity is irritating and exciting to the body.
19. Positive energy is sedative and relaxing.
20. Some colors advance and others recede. Orange, red, and yellow are advancing colors and they make a room seem smaller. Purple, blue, violet and green are receding colors, and they make a room seem larger.
21. Blue is helpful in myopia physically and psychologically, for it draws the ego outward, makes the individual field-oriented so that he moves in harmony with his environment. Red is helpful in presbyopia or far-sighted individuals; it helps the person to become egocentric. Red in this case draws the ego back into the self. This person is too field-oriented and not sufficiently ego-centric. Blue is used for the introvert to come out of his shell. Blue deflects the forces of the head downward. Red sends the forces from the lower parts of the organism upward. The diaphragm is the regulator and distributor of both these forces: upward and downward.
22. Color blended with white becomes a tint.
23. The effect of color as heat; Color increases or decreases the temperature of a room; elevates or lowers temperature; repels or concentrates rays.

24. Color has other powerful effects on the bodily functions which are both mental and physical in nature. Many of these have yet to be investigated; but some are known as will be seen below.
25. Retinal reactions to color have a vital effect on the nervous system.
26. Color develops ionization which is vital for life.
27. The skin has the property (selectivity of the cells) of selecting such color as it needs—either normally or when abnormal process is going on in the body.

Both processes can and do go on at the same time. The tissue changes the light emanation to meet its special requirements. According to Dr. George Stan White, an early pioneer in chromotherapy, these facts were to be noted:

a)   A change takes place in the character of the light energy being passed through the organism.

b)   The energy that passes into the body is not the same as the energy that contacts the skin. Skin is a natural filter and produces change.

c)   The resultant energy passing into the body after being filtered by the skin is to some extent absorbed by the body fluids, the extent of the absorption depending on the proportion of irritating and non-irritating compounds. It is the latter that is absorbed.

d)   It is **the energy resultant that is important in healing** and not the radiant energy of various frequencies that is thought to be important.

e)   "Radiant Energy Resultant that is absorbed internally differs with the source of the energy and also differs with the type of filters used. Light is a natural food and radiant energy is a catalytic agent, causing the body to take from other food that which it would not obtain were the radiant energy not administered." Skin pores close when subjected to a steady flow of strong light or radiant energy.

28. Radiant colors have an effect on motion:
Radiant color provides a means of differentiating rate and

modes of motion more subtle than any instrument. This is so because radiant color interferes with or neutralizes any energy acting upon a vital energy force, just as one wave will neutralize another wave of equal force and magnitude. All healing agents and methods must have for their goal the normalizing of an abnormal rate and mode of motion.

29. Author's theory to explain radiant colors:

When a complementary color is applied to a diseased area, the complementary color interferes with the disease radiations and produces a temporary balance. This temporary balance may give the appearance of a cure for that disease. In reality, it is the same disease in a different disguise because the cause is the same. Where the strainer is not removed, the healer is treating symptoms. [This temporary cure or manifestation is due to the synchronization of the complementary color with the vibration of the organs in the body which also has its normal determined frequency range.] Where the strainer is removed and normal vibration re-established, the conservatism of the body asserts itself, and the organism tends to remain in the fixed pattern which is called health. With the removal of the strainer, the organism returns to its normal frequency range or health since any vibration outside the normal determined frequency range is disease.

30. The color the object appears to have is the color which the object cannot absorb. The color the eye sees is that which is being thrown off or is being rejected.

31. How to see the complementary colors: To see the complementary colors, look at a colored object for a short time and then look quickly at a white surface. An image of the object will appear, but in the color complementary to that of the actual value. This will be the exact color value of the original hue, but it will gradually become lighter.

The image will vanish in a short time, but will reappear in an altered hue. This secondary change may, at times, be useful in treatment. It is necessary to know the colors which are complementary to each other as opposites have a more powerful effect when used alternately.

Chart of Complementary Colors:

Red is complementary to
Blue   Yellow ... to Violet
Blue ... to Red   Orange ... to Violet
Violet ... to Yellow   Green ... to Magenta
Violet ... to Orange   Magenta ... to Green

D. Chemical-Physical Properties of Color

32. The chemical or electrical rays (actinic) are blue, violet, and ultra-violet.
33. The acid rays are chemical colors and substances in which the electrical forces are dominant: blue, violet, and ultra-violet are the chemical colors; blue is associated with cold.
34. The alkaline colors are of a thermal nature: expansive and relaxing in character. Red in nature is heat; red in disease is heat expressed as fever, redness, and inflammation. Psychologically speaking, red is the color of anger, blushing, and passion.
35. Color develops ionization which is vital for life.
36. There are affinities between the energies of certain colors having opposite attributes just as there are affinities between certain elements in chemistry.
37. Color has polarity.

E. Psychological Properties of Color

This analysis is presented in the section on **Diagnosis.**

CHAPTER V

THE HEALING POWERS OF THE INDIVIDUAL COLORS

Some Reminders about Color and Healing

1. Life is color: each organ has a specific color.
2. Each color has intelligence and polarity.
3. Each color knows its functional role and it works selectively.
4. Each color does its work individually and collectively.
5. The right color is the right food in the right place at the right time.
6. Man is color living on the forty-ninth vibration.

The individual colors will be detailed in inventory fashion as they apply to diseases, and their healing properties will be listed. But before they can be capsulated, certain aspects of physiology will be related for the vital role played by color vibration. Without color, there is death. With color, there is physiology. No mention is made of the different theories about the individual colors and their healing powers since the many opinions, like the multitudinous seas, have ebbed and flowed in the first part of this study. Specifically the nature of matter and its color equivalents, the use of color in metabolism and fever, the role of drugs as contrasted with the role of color will be recounted here and then focused against the back-drop of Rife's findings when, with his special technique, he showed how the micro-organism in its natural color changed its nature and form and transformed itself into a malignant or a harmless organism. What man searches for in healing is the discovery of a law that is as parsimoniously phrased and as accurate as Einstein's law of $E = MC^2$

In the author's opinion, all disease, other than congenital defects or injury from accidents, represents

The effect of imbalance of Color

1. Excess of color energy on one side of the spectrum.
2. Deficiency of color energy on one side of the spectrum.
    One and two above result from an imbalance between the energies from both sides of the spectrum.
3. Inability of the organism and its balancing mechanism to utilize or adjust to the colors of the spectrum.

Nature of Matter on the Forty-Ninth Vibration

Spectrum analysis shows that the elements have no "pure" color; therefore all elements are compounds and the purest element is color. Matter disintegrates and all matter radiates as a result of this disintegration process; light is a function of the disintegration of matter. The sun gives off no light (directly), but emits energies arising from combustion. These energies are converted into light **by friction** as they pass through the density of the atmosphere. Color is a divisional part of light: a narrow portion of the forty-ninth vibration.

Sound, heat, light, magnetism are all the same energy, differing only in frequency of vibration and the medium of conduction. All known energies are composed of oscillatory frequencies in different media of transportation, and all life (as contrasted to the matter in which life manifests itself) is composed of energies. Therefore it is easy to understand how the use of light reinforces the life energies of the human body through polarity.

Magenta (red and violet) has the same vibratory or oscillatory rate as green; yet the visible color is different from green and the effects on the body are also different.

The question then arises: how is it that two colors can be different and at the same time have the same vibratory rate? The answer is that the vibratory rate is not the only factor in color. The direction with respect to the plane of polarization is another important factor. In the case of magenta, it has the opposite direction of rotation from green. The chemical formula of carbon, coal, and the diamond is the same. The difference lies in the way the atoms are assembled together. The same atoms assembled in different sequence produce different results. Ghadiali states that green is the north pole of the body and magenta is the south pole. Both work together and cannot be isolated: like both poles of a magnet.

Drugs or Color for Healing

Thousands of drugs are used in medical practice today and one must question the wisdom of dumping these drugs into the human organism when the constituents of the drugs are not included in the natural composition of the body. There is no perceptible quantity of mercury in the body and yet, in the treatment of syphilis and other ailments, when mercury is administered in large quantities, medicine ignores the fundamental chemistry of the human being. Whatever benefit is obtained is the result of the color in the mercury: potency of turquoise in this instance. No part unrelated to the functioning of a machine can be shackled to it or shoveled into it without upsetting its rhythm. Chemicals are live potencies; their atoms have attraction and repulsion. To endeavor to introduce haphazard inorganic metals into an organic machine is like feeding steel tacks to a body to make it strong. Imbalance of an element in the body whether above or below its normal percentage is the prime cause of illness.

Here the author wishes to observe that physicians who increase the imbalance or lower it with their drugs thereby cause iatrogenic or doctor-induced disease:

a) Because drugs can be unreliable and leave side effects that are worse than the original disease: Example 1: atropine when used for relaxation of spasm produces the drying of the mucous membrane which is harmful to the body. Example 2: Thalidomide and its scandal.

b) Because of individual differences, certain people are bound to react violently to a drug with disastrous consequences, and others will not be affected by the same drug: Example is the reaction to penicillin.

c)   Because all drugs are toxic and act as strainers on the body.
d)   Because drugs may relieve a symptom and yet upset the balance of the body.

Color therapy, on the other hand, is not poisonous (there are no poisonous rays in the visible spectrum), leaves no injurious side effects, is not a strainer on the body, and goes directly to the fundamentals of illness to reestablish a balance among the vibrating energies of the body. These vibratory energies activate all the different organs, glands, and systems of the body. An interesting analogy of importance to healing must be noted. Color matches the constituents of the auric bodies which, in turn, need low power and a high rate of vibration, two qualities that color supplies. Here it may be added that chemical reactions are crude vibrations and are ineffectual if not actually injurious to the auric bodies. One basic rule to be remembered:

Chemical reactions in the body act in arithmetic ratio.
Color reactions in the body act in geometric ratio.

One of the great pioneers, Dr. Babbitt, on publishing his research in color devised a pharmacopoeia that any who wish to know the scientific application should consult to speculate on what role color will play in medicine when drugs stop acting the stellar parts that allopathic medicine has cast for them. Babbitt's book may be called the **Gray's Anatomy of Color.**

Recapitulation:

1.   The vibratory essence of a drug, chemical, or element is represented in the color thrown off when that drug, chemical or element is disintegrating.
2.   Corresponding therapeutic effects are obtainable from using the color that correlates with the element in which the body is deficient or which has an affinity reaction with the element with which the body is over-supplied.

3. The different color represents energies required by the human body for its proper functioning.
4. The light rays are absorbed by the auric bodies of man through which the remedial effects on the physical body are obtained.

Metabolism and Color

Metabolism is essential to life and is a balance between the two processes—anabolism and catabolism. Anabolism is the building process by which energy is produced, tissue created and maintained, and damage to the cell repaired. Catabolism is the opposite process and is necessary to keep growth from running wild, to maintain the shape and integrity of the organism, and to eliminate waste from the body. In degenerate diseases, anabolism is weak and catabolism is strong; the result is that the tissue repair is inadequate and the organ degenerates. In toxic diseases, catabolism is deficient with the result that toxic or waste substances accumulate in the body and may poison the entire system. In tumors, benign and malignant, anabolism is excessive and catabolism is low; the growth principle is high and out of control and the shape and function of the body are changed. Anarchy reigns. Health is the proper balance between the two processes.

Ghadiali's book entitled **Spectro-Chrome-Metry Encyclopedia** is the **materia medica** of color. He states that the color red or anabolic is constructive and activates the liver. Violet or catabolic is destructive and activates the spleen. Red blood corpuscles are constant and are produced in the bone marrow with the aid of certain secretions from the liver. Worn out red corpuscles are destroyed in the spleen. White cells or phagocytes are produced in the spleen and destroy bacteria, a cause of infections according to germ theory adherents. Red and violet are the opposite ends of the spectrum (Yin and the Yang). Green which activates the pituitary is the balance between the liver and the spleen, and the pituitary regulates metabolism. For each organ and system of the body, there is a particular color that stimulates and another color that inhibits the action of that organ or system.

Metabolism, Fever, and Color

Before any premises may be drawn about how color affects fever, the reader must recall that fever is a normal process in the body for the functioning of metabolism and that fever is a method of re-establishing body equilibrium.

In all types of fever, there is a predominance of hydrogen and carbon in the body, chemical elements which fall on the hot side of the spectrum—the spectroscopic color of hydrogen is red and of carbon is yellow. To reduce the fever, one must burn out the excess of hydrogen and carbon, a process which requires oxygen, the spectroscopic color of which is blue. Blue light soothes and heals fevers and all inflammatory conditions. Oxygen unites with the hydrogen to form water, a neutral compound which is eliminated through the skin, breath, and kidneys; and oxygen unites with carbon to form carbon dioxide which is eliminated from the body via the lungs. This blue oxygen energy has the effect of extracting or neutralizing the excessive hydrogen and carbon (red and yellow) rays from the body. Extraction here is the affinity principle. There are affinities between the energies of certain colors having opposite attributes, just as there are affinities between certain elements which result in their combination into compounds. Affinity in chemistry refers to attraction. In chromotherapy, affinity waves have opposite attributes or qualities. Hence they seek one another to combine or to neutralize.

The Royal Raymond Rife Microscope and Color Findings

By heterodyning light through his microscope, a remarkable technique, Royal Raymond Rife was able to see without the use of a stain or dye, in the living state and in the natural color the vibrating micro-organism. The technique will revolutionize bacteriology, but here the application of his research must be stressed. He reports that when two different frequencies of vibration are produced, they interact upon one another to produce two new frequencies—one of which is the sum of the two original or fundamental frequencies; the other is the difference between the two originating or fundamental frequencies. Example: 500 and 600 sum: 1100; difference 100.

Further, in reporting on the frequency characteristic of micro-organisms, he showed how each type of bacteria and virus has its own characteristic color-life frequency vibration. When one turns the microscope to its own frequency of light, the micro-organism becomes brilliantly visible without the use of any chemical stain. Bacillus Typhus is blue; Bacillus Coli is mahogany; Mycobacterium Liprae is always ruby shade, etc. Rife reports further that the cancer virus, which he terms **BX** can become, with a slight change in the chemical media for the culture, another virus, which he named **BY.** Another slight change in the chemical media, and the virus is transformed into a monocyte fungibacilius Coli. If the Coli is kept in a certain machine for a year, the time required for metastasis—the virus reappears as **BX,** the cancer virus. The change in the chemical environment required to effect these transformations is very slight; in fact, it is stated that an alteration of four parts per million in the media will transform the harmless **B** Coli into a deadly **B** Typhosus within 48 hours (this supports Bechamp).

Interpretation of the Rife Findings

Rife divides all pathogenic micro-organisms into ten groups. Any micro-organism can be converted into that of any other within that group by changing the chemical environment sometimes by as little as two parts per million. Thus **it can be seen how slight are the metabolic changes in the body tissues that can induce a micro-organism of one color in one group to change into another micro-organism with a different color in the same group.** Rife's findings show that the change in the environment changes the frequency, which changes the color vibration and thus changes the organism. The organism goes from one to another vibration.

Under the Universal Rife microscope, one can readily see how an organism succumbs when exposed to certain lethal frequencies peculiar to that organism. A very effective ray is color. Each micro-organism has its own particular life frequency or rate of vibration in the light band; the logical corollary is that for each type of micro-organism, there is also some frequency radiation or rate of oscillation that will be destructive to the micro-organism.

Light is a vibratory radiation. Visible light is the oscillating band corresponding to the forty-ninth vibration. Each succeeding higher vibration has twice the vibrations per second of the first four vibrations of the second; eight vibrations of the third; sixteen of the fourth; thirty-two of the fifth; and so on up the scale. The difference between the colors of visible light lies in their vibratory rate:

a) Red, the color with the lowest vibratory rate, has an oscillatory rate of 436 trillion times per second.
b) Violet, the color with the highest rate, has an oscillation of 731 trillion times per second.

Significance of Rife's Findings for Color Healing

1. Light as man sees it is a vibration on the forty-ninth level.
2. Color is very effective in healing because it maintains the balance of the body; any change in environment is disease.
3. Color can re-establish the right frequency when there is too much or too little vibration in the body.
4. Color is the natural food of the body because the food derived from the plant is nothing but color in a solid form; animals are parasitic for their food is derived from plant life.
5. Cancer and other diseases are reversible and can be cured with the proper type of vibrations and with the proper nutrition.

The Warm Colors of the Spectrum: Red, Yellow, and Orange—Used Interchangeably

Red

1. Red is the element of fire. Fire is important for all living things; without fire, cold would paralyze everything; without heat, no motion or activity would be possible.
2. Red stimulates and excites the nerves and the blood.
3. Red stimulates the sensory nerves; therefore it is of benefit in deficiencies of smell, sight, hearing, taste and touch.
4. Red activates the circulation of the blood, excites the cerebro-spinal fluid and sympathetic nervous systems.
5. Red is a hemoglobin builder.
6. Red rays produce heat which vitalizes and energizes the physical body.
7. Red is a liver energizer.
8. Red is good for the muscular system and the left cerebral brain hemisphere.
9. Red is a counter-irritant, and its heat is excellent for contracted muscles.
10. Red rays decompose the salt crystals in the body and act as a catalyst for ionization. Without the process of ionization, nothing could be absorbed in the body. These ions are the carriers of the electro-magnetic energy in the body.
11. Red splits the ferric salt crystals into iron and salt with the red blood corpuscles absorbing the iron and then the salt's being eliminated by the kidneys and the skin.
12. Red rays liberate heat and clear congestion as well as the mucous.
13. Red, from a psychological viewpoint, represents health, fire, heat blood, anger, temper, danger and destruction. It stimulates, excites, and acts as an irritant. It gives man a sense of power.

Red is helpful for the presbyopic or far-sighted individual to help him become ego-centered. Red in this case draws the ego back into the self; this person is too field-oriented and not sufficiently egocentric. Red is used for the extrovert to go back into his shell.

Diseases Treated with Red

Anemia
Blood ailments
Bronchial Asthma
Bronchitis
Coccygeal area at the base of the spine (coccygeal Chakra). Red rays stimulate this area and cause the hemoglobin and corpuscles to multiply in the blood; red rays control the body temperature, and red affects the endocrine system through the coccygeal area
Cold—use red if there is no fever present
Constipation
Endocrine System— important; in addition to its role in stress, it plays a vital part in the health of the individual—physically, mentally, emotionally, and spiritually
Idiocy
Listlessness
Morons, imbeciles and idiots should be treated by Red
Melancholia
Paralysis
Physical Debility
Pneumonia
Tuberculosis

Red is contra-indicated in the following:

Emotionally disturbed people
Excitable temperaments
Fever
Florid complexioned people
Hypertension
Inflammatory conditions
Insanity—avoid red in most cases of insanity and emotional disturbances with the exception of catatonic patients.
Neuritis—An inflammation of the nerve.
Red-Headed individuals

Caution: If red is used too much and too often, it may produce fever and exhaustion; it should in most cases be used in conjunction with blue rays.

Yellow

Yellow activates the motor nerves; therefore it generates energy for the muscles. Disturbance in the supply of yellow energy to any part of the body can cause disturbance of function in that area including partial or complete paralysis; the basic cause is the deficiency of sensory and/or motor energy. Yellow being a mixture of red and green rays has half the stimulating potency of red and half the reparative potency of the green or nitrogen vibration; thus it tends both to stimulate function and to repair damaged cells. Yellow light directed at the intestinal tract for short periods is a digestant. For longer periods, it acts both as catharsis and as a cathartic. It also stimulates the flow of bile and has an anthelmintic action (antagonistic to parasites and worms).

1. Yellow is excellent for the nerves and the brain; is a motor stimulant and a nerve builder.
2. Yellow rays carry positive magnetic currents which strengthen the nerves and aid the brain.
3. Yellow has a stimulating, cleansing, and eliminating action on the liver, intestines, and the skin; it energizes the alimentary tract.
4. Yellow purifies the blood stream; it activates the lymphatic system.
5. Yellow is a spleen depressant, cathartic, cholegogue, anthelmintic.
6. Yellow is good psychologically for despondent and melancholy conditions. To the ancients, yellow was the animating color for life; it suggests joy, gaiety, merriment. It is the color of the intellect, of perception rather than of reason.

Diseases treated with Yellow

Constipation: use thirty minutes of yellow breathing or apply yellow rays on the navel. If the effect proves over-laxative, use a glass of blue solarized water or a blue light as a counter-measure.

Diabetes

Digestive Processes: Yellow controls the solar plexus (third chakra) area and the digestive processes; Yellow is used in gastro-intestinal cases

Eczema

Flatulence

Hemiplegic: Treat lumbar area in addition to paralysis treatment cited below.

Kidney

Indigestion

Liver

Mental/depression and exhaustion

Paralysis—since this is a disease of incoordination of brain, muscle, and nerve, use yellow over the occiput and the cervix.

Paraplegic: see paralysis, hemiplegic treatments above; add the sacral region and make sure to treat each sciatic nerve

Piles.

Rheumatism

Solar Plexus—Yellow controls the solar plexus (Third Chakra) area

Spleen

Yellow is contra-indicated in the following:

Acute inflammation
Delirium
Diarrhea
Fever

Neuralgia
Over-Excitement
Palpitation of the heart

Orange

Orange is a combination of red and yellow rays, and its healing power is greater than the two individual colors. As a color half way between red and yellow, it stimulates the thyroid gland, is a respiratory stimulant, but a depressant of parathyroid action. The parathyroid is opposite in function to the thyroid; and in good health there is a proper balance between the thyroid and the four small parathyroids. This relationship controls breathing. The orange vibration expands the lungs; the indigo vibratory impulse of the parathyroid contracts the lungs. The thyroid with its orange activity accentuates the hydrocarbon side of human chemistry through oxidation. For hypothyroidism, use orange. For hyperthyroidism, use indigo since indigo is both a thyroid depressant and activator of the parathyroid glands which work in opposition to the thyroid.

1. Orange has an antispasmatic effect; use orange for muscle spasms or cramps of all kinds.
2. The spectroscopic color of calcium is orange.
3. Orange aids the calcium metabolism of the body and strengthens the lungs.
4. Orange is indicated in abnormal putrefaction of the stomach, and it can have an emetic effect.
5. Orange stimulates the milk producing action of the breast after child birth.
6. Orange stimulates and increases the pulse rate, but does not affect the blood pressure.
7. Orange acts on the spleen and the pancreas to help assimilation and circulation.
8. Orange—its psychological effects:
   a) Orange combines physical energy with mental qualities.
   b) Orange releases the energy from both chakras of the spleen and the pancreas.
   c) Orange is the color for ideas and mental concepts.
   d) Orange strengthens the **etheric body,** enlivens the

emotions, and creates a general sense of well-being and cheerfulness.

   c)   Orange symbolizes warmth and prosperity.

9.   Orange is the color of heat, fire, will, and temporal power.

Diseases Treated with Orange

Asthma

Bronchitis

Chronic conditions like
  Asthma and Rheumatism

Colds

Epilepsy

Gall stones

Gout

Growths—malignant and
  non-malignant. Orange
  is indicated in all growths.
  In the precancerous stage,
  orange will often abort
  the condition. Where
  malignancy is suspected,
  orange is indicated with
  its complementary colors
  violet and purple.

Hyper-Hypothyroidism

Lung condition

Malignancy—see Growths
  above

Mestruation—cessation

Mental exhaustion

Kidney ailments

Prolapsus

Tumors—see Growths

Rheumatism

The Mid-Way Color on the Spectrum: Green

Green is the color of nitrogen which is the largest component of the atmosphere; it builds muscles, bones and other tissue cells.

1. Green is a negative color neither acid nor alkaline and can be used where blue is beneficial.

2. Green is cooling, soothing, and calming both physically and mentally. On exhausted men, green has at first a beneficial effect, but after a time, it becomes tiring.

3. Green acts upon the sympathetic nervous system; it relieves tension in the blood vessels and lowers the blood pressure.
4. Green dilates the capillaries and produces a sensation of warmth.
5. Green is an emotional stabilizer and pituitary stimulant.
6. Green acts upon the nervois system as a sedative and is helpful in sleeplessness, exhaustion, and irritability.
7. Green is thought to be the color of Vitamin B1.
8. Green is a muscle and tissue builder.
9. Green is an aphrodisiac and a sex tonic.
10. Green is a disinfectant, germicide, antiseptic and bacteriocide.
11. Green—its psychological effects:
    a) Green is emotionally soothing. In emotional disturbances, treat head with green.
    b) Green loosens and equalizes the etheric body.
    c) Green is the color of energy, youth, growth, inexperience, fertility, hope, and new life.
    d) Green is the color of envy, jealousy, and supersitition.

Diseases Treated with Green

Asthma
Back disorders—green is
  used over the small
  and lower back
Cold in the head
Colic
Erysipelas
Exhaustion
Hay fever
Heart conditions
Hepatic ailments
High blood pressure
Irritability
Laryngitis
Malaria

Malignancy—use solarized
  water and green light.
Nervous system
Nervous diseases
Neuralgia
Overstimulation
Piles
Shell shock
Sleeplessness
Syphilis
Typhoid
Ulcers
Venereal diseases

The Cold Colors of the Spectrum:
Blue, Indigo, and Violet

(Used Interchangeably—"Electric" colors of Soothing Effect)

Blue

1. Blue rays increase metabolism and build vitality.
2. Blue rays promote growth.
3. Blue rays slow the action of the heart and are therefore good for tachycardia.
4. Blue acts specifically on the blood and has a tonic effect.
5. Blue has antiseptic properties and is bacteriocidal; thereby it lessens and controls suppuration.
6. Blue is cold, electrical, and has contracting potencies.
7. Blue contracts the arteries, veins, and capillaries and thereby raises the blood pressure.
8. Blue is anticarcinogenic.
9. Blue rays are very fine and penetrating and excellent for inflammatory diseases, on which they have a soothing and cooling effect.
10 Blue is the balancing and harmonizing color to return the blood streem to normal when the blood becomes over-active and inflamed.
11. Blue reduces nervous excitement.
12. Blue is cooling, soothing, and astringent.
13. Blue—its psychological effects:
    a) Blue is good for over-excitement.
    b) Blue is good in cases of the manic depressive—for the manic phase (and red in the depressive phase).
    c) Blue is more soothing than green in emotional conditions.
    d) Blue is the color for meditation and spiritual expansion.
    e) Blue relaxes the mind and controls the throat chakra, which is the creative power center.
    f) Blue is helpful in myopia physically and psychologically for it draws the ego outward, making the individual field-oriented and more in harmony with his environment.

g) Blue is used for the introvert to come out of his shell.

h) Blue rays: it has been found that after ten minutes of treatment with blue rays, most people tire and begin to feel depressed.

i) Blue clothing and blue furnishings if not broken up with other colors make one tired and depressed.

j) Blue is the color for truth, devotion, calmness, and sincerity.

k) Blue is the color of intuition and the higher mental faculties.

Diseases Treated with Blue

Apoplexy

Baldness—in a number of cases, baldness has responded to blue light on the scalp for fifteen minutes a day

Biliousness

Bowels

Bubonic plague

Burns

Cataracts and glaucoma— have patient gaze into blue light for thirty minutes each day

Chicken pox

Cholera

Colic

Diarrhea

Dysentery

Eye-inflammation

Epilepsy

Febrile diseases

Gastro-Intestinal disease

Hydrophobia—treat with blue light two to three hours daily and have patient drink solarized water

Hysteria

Insomnia

Itching

Jaundice

Laryngitis—can be healed by drinking half a glass of blue solarized water every half hour and gargling with the other half of blue solarized water; or use blue light on throat

Measles

Menstruation—painful

Palpitation

Polio—use blue light on the spine for thirty minutes, three times daily

Glaucoma—see Cataracts
Goitre
Gonorrhea—responds favorably
  to blue light.
Headache
Renal Diseases
Rheumatism—acute
Scarlet fever
Shock
Skin
Syphilis—responds favorably
  to blue light
Teeth
Throat trouble—all tonsilitis
Typhoid Fever

Ulcers: Duodenal—treat with
  blue light over the duodenum
  for thirty minutes
Gastric: treat with yellow
  light on abdomen for forty
  five minutes and then with
  blue or ultra-violet light for
  fifteen minutes
Vomiting
Whooping cough

Blue is contra-indicated for the following:

Colds
Constrictuion of muscles
Gouth
Hypertension

Muscles—constriction
Paralysis
Rhematism—chronic
Tachycardia

Indigo

1. Indigo is electric, cooling and astringent.
2. Indigo is a parathyroid stimulant; a thyroid depressant.
3. Indigo is a purifier of the blood stream.
4. Indigo is a phagocyte builder in the spleen.
5. Indigo is hemostatic (helps reduce or stop excessive bleeding).
6. Indigo is good for muscular tonicity.
7. Indigo is a respiratory depressor.
8. Indigo can be effective as an anethetic and can induce total in-
   sensibility.
   This is not a form of hypnosis, for the patient retains all his
   physical and mental faculties and there is no after-effect. The

patient keeps looking at indigo, through colored lenses for the time necessary to become insensible to pain without losing consciousness. The indigo seems to raise the consciousness of the patient to such a high level of vibration that he becomes unaware of the physical body.

9. Indigo—its psychological effects:
    a) Indigo controls the psychic currents of the subtle bodies.
    b) Indigo governs the chakra in the centre of the forehead—called the spiritual or the third eye—controlling the pineal gland.
    c) Indigo affects vision, hearing, and smell on the physical, emotional, and spiritual plane.
    d) Indigo: visual purple or rhodopsin is necessary in vision to distinguish form and objects, and its color is thought to be indigo.

Diseases Treated with Indigo:

Appendicitis

Asthma

Bronchitis

Cataracts—treat with light and solarized water; advisable for patient to wear a transparent eye-shade of the color indigo

Convulsions

Delirium Tremens or

Delirium Tremors

Dyspepsia

Ear-deafness—orange and indigo should be used alternatively

Ear difficulties—if inflamed use blue; then follow with indigo and solarized water

Hyperthyroidism

Insanity

Lung trouble—all

Nervous ailments

Nasal diseases

Nose Bleed—use indigo light and solarized water

Nose ailments

Obsession

Palsy

Paralysis—facial

Pneumonia—responds best to indigo unless there is a hemorrhage of the lungs; then blue should be used

Smell—for an improvement in the sense of smell, use pink; then indigo

Ear diseases—if abnormal
   sounds in the ear, due to
   heat, then use indigo
   light on head
Eye diseases

Throat diseases
Tonsillitis
Whooping cough

Violet

1. Violet stimulates the spleen.
2. Violet is both a motor nerve and lymphatic depressor.
3. Violet is a cardiac depressor.
4. Violet nourishes the blood in the upper brain.
5. Violet purifies the blood; it is a leucocyte builder.
6. Violet maintains the potassium and sodium balance of the body (Tumors cannot grow in a potassium medium).
7. Violet is good for bone-growth.
8. Violet—its psychological effects: Excellent in calming or overcoming the excesses of violent insanity; it controls irritability in the sane; controls excess hunger.
    a) Violet is an inspiring and spiritual color. Leonardo da Vinci said, "The power of meditation can be ten times greater under violet light falling through the stained glass window of a quiet church."
    b) Violet is a healing color. Comte Saint Germain healed with violet rays. In Eastern philosophy, violet is the ruler of the centre of the head, and this is called the Thousand-Petalled Lotus.

Diseases Treated with Violet

Bladder trouble
Bone growth
Cerebro spinal meningitis
Concussion
Cramps
Epilepsy
Kidneys
Leucoderma
Mental disorders

Neuralgia
Nervous disorders
Rheumatism
Sciatica
Scalp diseases
Skin
Tumors

Ultra-Violet

1. Ultra-violet has a chemical and bacteriocidal action on the blood and tissues of the body.
2. Ultra-violet's chemical reaction depends upon its vitamin reaction in the system, and Vitamins A,B,C,D, and E are, in turn, affected by the ultra-violet light. There is an inter-relationship between these rays and these vitamins.
3. Ultra-violet plays a great part in the calcium phosphorus balance and in iron and iodine fixation; for that reason, it is good in the treatment of rickets and goiters.
4. Ultra-violet breaks down bacterial toxins and helps the white blood cells in their phagocytic action.
5. Ultra-violet accelerates the lymphatic and circulatory activities.
6. Ultra-violet normalizes all metabolism and glandular activities.
7. Ultra-violet stimulates antibody production and immunizes the body against disease.
8. Ultra-violet has a stimulating action on the Sympathetic System; yet acts as a sedative to pain.
9. Ultra-violet is good for the heart and the lungs.

Diseases Treated with Ultra-Violet

Goiter	Rickets
Gonorrhea	Syphilis
Heart	Ulcer
Lungs	Wounds

Color not on the Visible Spectrum: Lemon, Purple, Turquoise, Magenta, Scarlet

Lemon: Combination of yellow and green

Lemon

1. Lemon is a cerebral stimulant.
2. Lemon under spectroscopic analysis poses many aspects pertinent for color healing. It must be noted that phosphorus and sulphur stimulate the brain; both phosphorus and sulphur are lemon under the spectroscope. Gold and silver likewise give a lemon color under the spectroscope. Gold in the male and silver in the female are the yin and yang variants of polarity, and they provide a lemon vibration on the spectroscope. Lemon is a sexual stimulant (there is more to giving a woman a gold necklace than appears in Tiffany's catalogue).
3. Lemon activates the thymus gland and thus controls growth.

    Ghadiali states that the thymus gland located in the upper chest at birth contains uranium in its composition. The thymus is a regulator of physical growth and maturation. He further states that the growth process is due to the slow disintegration of uranium which produces the chemical necessary to the growth of the body. When the store of uranium in the thymus is used up, no further appreciable growth in the body can occur (The author has called this deposit of uranium a "growth bomb" or the "built-in time clock")
4. Lemon being half green has the effect of a cleanser of the system, and being half yellow also has the effect of a motor stimulant to throw off morbid debris. In case of coughing, there is need to throw off phlegm. This requires motor stimulation. Yellow and green are both cleansers and lemon has the quality of both.

Diseases Treated with Lemon

Bone builder—strengthens bone

Bone growth (Phosphorus has lemon vibration on

Chronic conditions—Lemon, like the fruit has an antacid

Cleanser of the system

Coughing: use lemon as irradiative agent over the the affected area

Cretinism and dwarfism—in view of its effects in

effect on the body, excellent for chronic conditions. It gives energy to the cells in the stage of resistance and exhaustion and helps overcome stress

stimulating the thymus gland

Motor stimulant

Purple (including Scarlet)

Purple is a combination of red and blue. Scarlet and purple have opposite effects: scarlet is a vasoconstrictor and raises the blood pressure while purple is a vasodilator and lowers the blood pressure (see Magenta).

1. Scarlet stimulates kidney activity and the sexual mechanism.
2. Scarlet helps in cases of impotency and frigidity when used in the genital area.
3. Scarlet is indicated for scant menstruation.
4. Purple is used in excessive menstruation, for it is opposite in effect to scarlet; in severe cases of excessive bleeding, indigo should be substituted for purple because of its property: to reduce bleeding.
5. Purple has an analgesic, anti-pyretic, narcotic and hypnotic effect; and to achieve these purposes, purple can be used with a long exposure.
6. Purple is indicated in malaria.
7. Purple is the color of anger, divinity and royalty.
8. Purple is to be used where animation without irritation is needed.
9. Purple is a venous stimulant.

Diseases treated with Purple

Body distresses where animation is needed without irritation
All parts of the body where this need is dictated.

Kidneys

Lungs

Stomach—if stomach is hot and excitable, use purple. If stomach is upset, but without inflammation, use red-purple.

Turquoise

It combines the cleansing action of green and the soothing action of blue. In treating febrile diseases, change to turquoise when the temperature is normal.

1. Turquoise has the opposite effect of lemon; it is acid and tonic in its action.
2. Turquoise is a prime skin-building color and should be used after the pain from burns is relieved. Turquoise hastens the formation of new skin.
3. Turquoise is a cerebral depressant for over-active mental patients.

Magenta

1. Magenta energizes the adrenal glands, the heart action and the reproduction system.
2. Magenta acts as a diuretic.
3. Magenta is good for the treatment of the auric bodies.
4. Magenta is a fine emotional stabilizer.

Scarlet

1. Scarlet is an arterial stimulant and a renal energizer.
2. Scarlet is a genital excitement, an emmenagogue which promotes menstrual discharge, a vasoconstrictor. An ecbolic, and a sex builder in those with subnormal sex potency.

CHAPTER VI

DIAGNOSIS OF DISEASE

Diagnosis in color requires training and experience as all disciplines dictate. One proceeds on the premise that visible light affects the individual physically, emotionally, and mentally. Apart from vision, color biologically affects growth, the healing of wounds, lactation, muscular tension and the following systems: the nervous, the endocrine, the digestive, the reproductive, and the circulatory—in short the entire body. On this premise, one diagnoses the physical, the emotional, as well as the psychosomatic responses.

As a general rule, there are two methods used in diagnosis:— 1. Seeing the cause. 2. Detecting the symptoms. The following techniques will utilise these two methods.

i. Observation	v. Psychological diagnosis
ii. Pulse test	vi. Visualization techniques
iii. Short leg test	vii. Prism diagnosis
vi. Aura, electromagnetic diagnosis	viii. Radionics technique

Diagnosis by Observation:

For one trained in Western ways of allopathic medicine, the observation of color of the various organs of the body in determining the diagnosis is more honored in the breach, than in the observing. The Chromotherapist, on the other hand, has developed the technique of observation to a highly refined art and the patient is usually amazed with the results. Twelve different parts of the body will be detailed with the significance the color reveals of internal disease and then an explanation will be provided of how the reflexes inter-relate by way of color or sound the different parts of the body from the skin inward.

1. The color of the eye can reveal seventy-two different eye troubles. Iris diagnosis is a specialist's technique in Western medicine requiring years of study, but the Chinese from the Ting Dynasty to the present, made eye diagnoses part of every physician's equipment.[1] The red in the large corner of the eye nasally signifies a strong heart; red in the small corner of the eye next to the cheek, temple side, reveals a weak heart.

    The eyeball colors are related to the liver and the pupil to the condition of the kidneys. The whites of the eye (Sclera) to the lungs, and the upper and the lower lids of the eyes to the stomach.

2. The color of the nails reveals, among other things, the condition of the liver. This should always be checked with the eyes. The nails reveal the nutritional and emotional state of the body. The Turkish doctor, not allowed to enter the harem, examined the hand extended through the opening of a curtain to determine illness from the color and shape of the finger nails, and he became very expert.

3. The color of the urine: A light yellow indicates it is normal; a dark color, toxins and poisons; bloody, inflammation of the bladder, decay of the kidneys, or a prostate condition in the male; malignancy. White is an indication of weakness; yellow, of inflammation.

4. The color of the stools: Brown indicates the condition is normal; white indicates trouble in the liver, stomach or kidneys, darkness indicates poisons or inflammation in the large intestines; black indicates internal bleeding—the blacker the color, the higher up in the body is the source of the trouble. When the bowels move regularly but a little at a time and cause cramps, colitis is present or there is trouble in the large intestines.

1. All organs are represented in the Iris of the eyes in well-defined areas. The iris of the eye is made up of a vast number of minute nerve filaments which through the optic nerve, optic thalmus and the spinal cord are connected with and receive impressions from every nerve in the body. The nerve filaments, muscle fibres, and minute blood vessels in the different areas of the iris reproduce the changing conditions in the corresponding parts or organs.

5. In looking at the color of the skin, observe the complexion, lips, eyes, hands, feet, and torso. From the color of the skin, one can observe if there are growths, lacerations, contusions, abrasions, and wounds present. In hypertension or in any other condition in which the skin's blood vessels are dilated, the skin is red. In anemia, it will be pale, due to the lower number of red blood corpuscles.

In heart disease and in respiratory ailments like bronchitis and pneumonia, the skin may appear purple because of improper oxygenation of the blood. In jaundice and in hepatitis, the skin will appear yellow because of increase in bilirubin in the blood stream. Diabetes Mellitus, Hemocromatosis or prolonged arsenic treatment may cause pigmentation of the skin. In pregnancy, there may be skin discoloration on the abdomen and around the nipples; in some cases, the whole body darkens, especially with brunettes. In Pellagra, there is darkening and pigmentation on the back of the hands, forearms, face and neck. Sunburn or scarlet fever is indicated by redness over a large area; a local inflammation is indicated by a redness over a confined area. Poor circulation is revealed by lack of color in the extremities.

Looseness of skin is a sign of poor tone at any age.

Tightness of skin may be the result of nervous tension, swelling, edema or growths.

Dry skin may be the result of age, detergents, itch, myxedema, scurvy, kidney trouble, exposure, or lack of Vitamin A.

Moist skin is a sign of excitement, emotional instability, fever or overheating.

Inelasticity of the tissues is a sign of atrophy.

A cold clammy hand is sign of poor peripheral circulation.

Shiny or thin skin around the joints is a sign of arthritis.

Profuse sweating may be due to excitement, pain, overheating, parasites, broken bone, tuberculosis, menopause, and certain conditions of pregnancy.

6. The color of the hair reveals the condition of the body and tells the practitioner a great deal about the kidneys. Color dyes cause different wave lengths to be absorbed by the skin

with different effects on the organism—from no reaction to death. It is known too that some of the coal dyes are carcinogenic.

7. The color of the lips indicates the condition of the stomach; if very red, the stomach is full of gas, fermentation, acids, and is inflamed; if white, the stomach is in a weak condition; if red, heat is indicated; if any dark color is shown, the condition is abnormal; if a dark color appears around the eyes, look for trouble in the kidney or liver. In the female, this condition is often caused by menstruation. If lips are blue or purplish, there is trouble with the heart or the circulatory system.

8. The color of the tongue may indicate as many as one hundred and twenty different conditions or symptoms. In most cases of disease, the tongue has a yellow or a white coating. The yellow color denotes a condition of inflammation. If the tongue is covered all over with yellow, the whole system is sluggish, and this condition always indicates constipation and toxicity. A white tongue denotes an absence of inflammation. If the tongue is smooth and dark red, the kidneys have almost ceased functioning and the condition is serious. A red tongue signifies inflammation in the system.

   The root of the tongue pertains to the kidneys; the sides, to the liver; the centre to the stomach; the tip, to the heart.

9. Hand color: As a general rule, the Chinese do not use the pulse[2] test for children under the age of five, but make their diagnosis from the condition of the fingers.

   A red color indicates a cold; purple, a fever or inflammation; blue, excitement or fear; a pale color, scurvy or anemia; a light yellow color is not serious, but a dark color is very dangerous. If this dark color spreads to the palm of the hand, the life of the child may end at any moment.

10. The ear is an organ for sound and equilibrium. Sound is another vibration and can be changed into color. The ear, like the eyes, contains hundreds of reflexes and thus narrates the

2. The Chinese and Indian taking of the pulse is an art and a science, and it tells the physician all about the major organs of the body. The technique is entirely different from the Western approach, and the two should not be confused.

story of body. The diagnosis and reflexes cannot be fully covered in this book, but examples will be cited below to show the subtle inter-relationship of the organs, the knowledge of which is necessary for any doctor's armortorium.

The ears are related to the kidneys. Wax, ringing in the ears, pus, the hardness of hearing, if physiological are all due to the malfunctioning of the kidneys. Itching at the back of the lobes or in the opening of the ear refers to an acid condition of the body or an inflamed kidney.

11. Complexion—Color and Organ-Relationship: The heart and circulation as well as the body's emotional state are revealed in the color of the complexion.
12. General Appearance: Gait, carriage, voice, and speech can give the diagnostician the physical and emotional picture of the patient. The face may show agitation, worry, depression, exhaustion, strain, emaciation, obesity and deformities. A marked loss of weight may signify an emotional problem, stomach pains, diabetes, malignancy, anemia or chemical poisoning. Chills may signify shock, malaria, kidney stones, drugs or the body's attempt to cleanse itself.

The above may well lead to a brief relating of the reflexes and how they diagnose the body's various ills.

The heart reflexes to the tongue and is related to the pulse. The condition of the liver is revealed in the tongue, eyes and nails, reflexes to the eyes and is related to the muscles. The stomach shows on the lips, reflexes to the tongue, opens to the nose, and relates to the flesh. The kidneys show in the hair, reflex to the sex organs, and relate to the nose. The lungs show in the pores, open to the nose and relate to the skin. The spleen relates to the stomach; the gall bladder, to the liver; the bladder, to the kidneys; the intestines, to the lungs.

All of these observations of the body should be taken into consideration as one alone might be deceptive.

II. Diagnosis by Pulse Test

The pulse should be taken before breakfast for three days preferably at the same hour each day until one knows his own pulse rate. One hour after each meal the pulse is taken; if the pulse rate goes up eight or more points, one or more of the foods or combination of the foods is bad for the individual. The individual must then go through a process of testing to eliminate what is harmful from his diet.

Every substance, whether food, furniture, housing, or thought, affects man. Wise is he who will use only those objects and foods that are beneficial to him and who will eliminate the other rays from his environment.

III. Diagnosis by Short-leg Test and its Relation to Allergies

All objects give off vibrations and color and affect the individual whether or not he knows it. If he is affected adversely, the diagnosis is made that he is allergic to that object. Allergies are nothing more than the violent reaction of the cells to an unpleasant stimulus. Pleasurable stimuli cause the cells to react from the centre to the periphery; the cell expands and grows. The leg gets longer. An unpleasurable stimulus causes the cell to react from the periphery to the centre. The cell contracts or withdraws; it becomes inhibited. It cannot grow. The leg gets shorter. It is out of harmony. If the strain or the unpleasant stimulus is not removed, altered function or pathology ensues or the cell dies.

Orthodox medicine has developed allergy tests which, in themselves, are unpleasant stimuli to the body. A much more rational test is the short leg test which gives excellent results, has no side effects, and does no damage to the body.

Short-leg Test: The reader is reminded of the reference in another part of this book to the statue of Buddha in Ceylon where the acute observation of this body muscle reaction was recorded in stone.

148

1. Patient is placed in the prone position with his face in the pillow and with soles of his feet extending over the bed. Make sure his shoes are removed.
2. Look to see that the patient is parallel to the bed.
3. Measure his legs to see which side is shorter. This is done merely by observation.
4. Most individuals have one side of the body shorter than the other.
5. If the legs are even, the person is in harmony.
6. Place the object to be tested in the hand of the patient.
7. If the shorter leg gets longer, the object is good for the individual.
8. If the shorter leg gets shorter, the object is unhealthy for the individual.

IV. Diagnosis by the 'Aura' or the Electro-Magnetic Field Test; Kilner Screen and Other Devices Dark-Room Technique

Place the patient in a dark room, preferably with dark walls or a dark curtain so that the radiation may be seen from the aura or electromagnetic force surrounding the entire body (like the halos around the heads of saints in medieval art). Since the aura has been photographed, there is evidence that it exists.

The healthy aura appears clear and bright, and the colors extend in waves several inches from the body. In ill health, the colors are dull and there are dark patches. The vibrations can usually be seen to curl inward over the affected part; this curling shows the location of the trouble. Kilner states that no two auras are alike. They change under various conditions of ill health, fatigue, and emotional disturbances. There is a close connection between the aura and the central nervous system. The shape and size of the aura change markedly in severe nervous disease. Its size and distinctiveness decrease in mental impairment.

Some times two or more auras can be seen: the one nearest the body is striated and called the inner aura; the other one, a wide amorphous part, is called the outer aura. The space between the inner aura and the body is called the **etheric double.**

In ill health, the aura frequently contains more yellow than normally is characteristic of it, and the yellow becomes especially pronounced in areas of local disturbances. This yellow is usually seen in patches in the midst of a blue complementary color band.

In a healthy person, the color of the complementary color band will be alike, or nearly so, on both sides of the body but in illness, one side may be darker than the other, the dark part usually lying over the affected part of the body. The affected part, however, may cause the complementary color band to appear lighter instead of darker. Sometimes a lighter or darker patch on the color band will occasionally take the shape of an organ or part of one. Smaller patches almost always point to the location of some pain or tenderness. Frequently a different colored spot will appear on the band, a spot that indicates the location of a previously sore area. This need not indicate anything abnormal.

The Aura and the Etheric Body
The author's Theory of the cause of Parkinson,
Muscular Dystrophy, and Multiple Sclerosis

Every individual is the product of his color responses and, according to Indian philosophy, is also the product of the various circumstances through which he has passed during the eons of time he has been an individualized soul. Man has seven subtle bodies, each of which radiates waves of color. The clairvoyant observes these colors without instruments and from them discerns in which of the subtle bodies the deficiency is located—thus showing the cause of illness. In the physiological sense, these subtle bodies can be broken down into chemical, electrical and other field forces of the body. The author considers Multiple Sclerosis, Muscular Dystrophy, and Parkinson—all diseases of the Electromagnetic forces of the body. The spiritual healer considers them diseases of the **Etheric Double.** It seems that the seven subtle bodies use the nerves of the physical body as transmitting and receiving centres to form a total organism which disintegrates on death. The same nerves conduct the impulses of the seven subtle bodies on different frequencies (this is done commercially by the telephone and the radio companies). Wherever necessary, the subtler body, less dense, sets up a collateral circuit by coming down a vibration to the frequency of the other, in order to preserve the total organism. These diseases may be due to the jamming of the frequencies.

V. Diagnosis by Psychological Tests

Anthropologists tell us that prehistoric man could not see colors: only black and white. The faculty to see color has developed slowly and is still developing. Today there is a certain percentage of the population that is color blind, and there are, on the other hand, individuals with a sense of sight far more keenly developed than is the average individual's. These people can see the aura, the electro-magnetic field force that surrounds the body.

It is essential to the diagnostician to know how people react to color, and the extremes of the insensitives and the sensitives become only one yardstick for gauging the so-called normal man. The diagnostician must also be aware that color affects man through the skin, the food, the emotions, and the sensory reactions. As a matter of fact, the emotional and the sensory reaction to color is accepted as an integral part of our culture, is reflected in our language, which is filled with many such recognitions.

This type of color reaction is becoming an accepted form of diagnosis for the emotionally disturbed.

Whether the emotional effect of color is a direct one or whether it is the outcome of association depends on the school of psychology one favors. It is known that a warm red color will excite while another shade of red will cause pain or disgust through the association with blood.

From the emotional view point—

1. Color has two divisions: warm-cold; light-dark.
2. Color has four shades of appeal: warm and light; warm and dark; cold and light; cold and dark.
3. Color has movement: warm color approaches the observer; dark color recedes from the observer; warm color moves out from the center and is field-oriented; cold color moves toward the center and is ego-centric.
4. Color is used in diagnosis of the mentally ill: the colors used and the forms drawn by the patient indicate mental and emotional health.

It is not the author's purpose, at this point, to discuss the various psychological tests. Many books are available on this interesting aspect of human development. What is basic to the analysis is to know that temperaments vary in their responsiveness to color and that these preferences have a psychological basis. Further, moods are associated with color as are thoughts and feelings, and this type of inter-relationship has been characteristic of man since the early days, so much so that color became a potent psychological force which through symbolism made a tremendous impact on man. A few of the symbolical interpretations of color will clarify this generalization. No references are made to mythology.

Colors and The Symbols

Red is the symbol of fire, passion, rage, danger, destruction. The Romans used a red flag in battle to stimulate the endocrine glands. This released adrenaline and helped increase the energy level. The Spartans used a blood-red flag in combat for the same reason. The Greek God of War Mars drove a red Chariot. Mephistopheles is always pictured in red. "He saw red" is said to indicate anger;
"A red-blooded man", to indicate a powerful man.
Yellow is the color of the intellect, of perception rather than of reason. Yellow if gazed at steadily has a disturbing influence.

To many of the ancients, it was the animating principle of life. To the Chinese, it symbolized nobility. It also suggests joy, gaiety, and merriment.

A murky yellow is associated with sickness, treason, and deception as well as cowardice: "a yellow streak", "yellow journalism."

Orange is the color of heat, fire, fever; it symbolizes warmth and prosperity.

Green is the color of hope, new life, energy, fertility, growth. Green is a restful color. On exhausted men, green has a beneficial effect but after a time it becomes wearisome. The term "greenhorn" means youth and inexperience. Dark green means envy, jealousy and supersitition: "green with envy."

Blue is the color of intuition and the higher mental faculties. It symbolizes true devotion, sincerity, and calmness: "true Blue." It is also the color of dejection and sadness: "feeling blue." It is used to signify loyalty and faithfulness, as in the American flag.

Purple is the color of dignity, majesty, and royalty: "royal purple." It is the color of rage: "purple with rage."

Black is the color denoting evil, fear, superstition, and destruction: "black magic," "black Sunday," "black despair," "black Friday."

White is the color signifying purity and goodness. It denotes something fearful—like the Albino White Whale Moby Dick. See this book for the many interpretations of white. It is the color of mourning for the Chinese.

To continue with the symbolism of color is unwise. Too much has been written on the subject for a synthesis to be attempted. The author has not avoided the matter in this section on diagnosis; instead he refers the reader here too, as he has in the matter of psychological tests, to the vast literature available. What is to be stressed is that in symbol and color, as in the analysis of dreams, is imbedded the race-wisdom and a history of man's characteristics on the mental, physical, and spiritual levels. The terms "Forgotten Language" and "Collective Unconscious" have been fittingly applied by Fromm and Jung to this aspect of human awareness and historical evolution.

How can the fact that color preferences have psychological bases be used in color therapy diagnosis?

1. Outward or field oriented people like warm colors.
2. Inward or ego-centered persons prefer the cool colors as they do not need the outer stimulation.
3. Emotionally responsive individuals react freely to color.
4. The emotionally inhibited person is often shocked by color (this color is driving me mad!) for it intrudes upon his inner life which he attempts to hide.
5. The emotionally indifferent or phlegmatic individual is usually a rigid personality and is unresponsive to and little affected by the finer vibrations of color.
6. From the view point of color, one may say that each color has its significance; as a general rule, the dark colors show depression and melancholy and the bright colors show gaiety and comedy. Any extremes in reaction to color are usually pathological.

The psychotherapist uses his training to study how temperaments vary in their responses to color and to determine how color preferences have a psychological basis. The colortherapist knows that there is not only an emotional reaction to color but also a physical reaction. The two interact: there is no such thing as a purely physical or a purely emotional illness. For this reason, color can be applied to healing all parts of the body by harmonizing the vibratory rate on the physical, emotional, and mental planes. Diagnosis must therefore measure these three planes.

VI. Diagnosis by Visualization

The technique of visualization devised by L.E. Eeman works on the principle of white light and respiration in this way:

1. The front of the subject's body is divided into seven equal parts to represent the colors of the spectrum: red at the top beginning at the base of the neck and violet at the bottom ending in the pelvic region.

2. The patient is asked to visualize the colors of the spectrum in their order—from red to violet.

3. If the patient's responses to the various colors are normal, the breathing will be smooth and regular from the upper portion of the chest and downward.

4. If the respiration is changed and is irregular because of the response to the color visualized, then look for the color that causes the change in body harmony. If the patient's responses to the color red, for example, increase the respiration in the upper chest, there is an imbalance in that area.

The Eeman technique is useful for diagnosis of a distressed area in the body if it is properly used. The physician who discovers the distressed area from the Eeman visualization technique may, however, be tempted to label the disease; for example, call the disease pneumonia or bronchitis. Here the reader is reminded that what is called disease is literally the absence of ease. The name of the disease is not important; for the disease could be any one of a multitude of warning flares called symptoms or distress signals which show the General Adaptation Syndrome at work. The physician could treat the body for bronchitis and then the body could send up a second warning: pneumonia. This type of particularization of the specific disease is not important to the colortherapist. He looks for the area that is out of balance and then he applies the complementary color to clear up the condition in the troubled area. Eeman simply says that the green rays may affect the epigastric area or the violet rays may produce deep abdominal breathing. But the author goes one step beyond to state: **Each organ has its own vibration and color. Treat the distressed area with its complementary color.**

VII. Diagnosis with a Prism

The prism is of invaluable assistance in diagnosis. To some authorities, it is a necessity. The prism in modern science is chiefly a medium of refraction, an important function. But in color therapy, the prism has a different use. The prism is a triangular piece made of either crown glass or flint. If sunlight is refracted through a prism, it splits up into seven clear colors: these can be shown on the screen and constitute the spectrum. This is Newton's classical experiment.

Various explanations of the phenomenon are given in scientific texts, but they do not explain why there are only seven colors and why the number is constant whenever sunlight is refracted. The scientists say merely that the white light of the sun is composed of seven colors called the visible spectrum. This is a statement—not an explanation. Why not turn this generalization about and say that these seven colors, real forces that one sees as well as reacts to everywhere, move in such a dimension that they are not perceptible to the ordinary eye. What man sees with the eyes is the effect of cosmic colors, but not the cosmic colors themselves: eg., man does not see electricity; he sees the effects of electricity.

The prism helps the eyes to adjust themselves to the dimension in which the cosmic colors move in the outside world to irradiate everything. These seven colored rays are according to some philosophers, the principal cosmic rays which, in a large measure, are responsible for creation, preservation, and the destruction of the universe (the Hindu triad of gods). They surround everyone and everything in this vast universe and give life, health, youth, old age, and death.

The table on page 80 is useful for prism analysis; it shows the connections among the elements, the sense organs, the senses, and the cosmic colors. The prism reveals the color of the afflicted organ, and one then applies the principle of complementarity.

VIII. Diagnosis by Radionics

This is an important area which will advance with time. Chief, among the many, is the De La Warr machine test, which diagnoses both the sub-atomic and the physical body through examining personal possessions or minute particles of the body. This has been explained in the chapter on theory in the other half of this study.

CHAPTER VII

TREATMENT:
PRINCIPLES AND TECHNIQUES

The physician healing with color must practice the principles herein enunciated, but first he must be sure he understands them with empathy. The colortherapist cannot afford to act as though he were a push-button technician or a chart reader of the spectroscope. He who combines a wise technique with an accurate knowledge of the reflexes, the nervous system, and the functions of each segment of the spinal cord as well as of the trigger points can perform wonders with colortherapy. First, however, he must know what colors should be used in treating the parts of the body, and he must have a thorough comprehension of the normal colors associated with what can be termed the healthy body parts. There is a dearth of accurate scientific information on this particular aspect of color-organ relation. Without a knowledge of the colors associated with the organs in conditions of health, the therapist cannot heal the sickness or the disease. Another aspect that he must be aware of relates to the new science in healing of medical radionics or distance therapy. The patient can be treated locally or from a distance. These principles are familiar from the widespread use of radio and television, but the applications to healing are yet to be promulgated. Distance-Therapy or color-in-Space Therapy is in its infancy, and the future will write the history of medical color radionics for color deals with life itself as the vital force in nature. This wise application of color ushering in health, emotional stability, and spiritual elevation banishes sickness, disease, affliction, and suffering. The how and the why are explained by the principles and the techniques of application.

Principles of Color Healing

Supplying chemicals is not the answer in overcoming diseases caused by such deficiencies; these are merely the raw materials. The chemicals must be supplied in the form by which they can be properly and most effectively utilized—and that form is color. The metal sheets must be molded and shaped to form a car. Ingots by themselves are useless. Color is the right form at the right time and in the right place. Color is the easiest element to be utilized by the body for its needs and is a perfect exemplification of the law of parsimony.

1. Supply the color the individual lacks or reduce a too-abundant color which is throwing the body out of balance. Neutralize the over abundant color by using its complementary shade.
2. Remember that red and blue are the two basics of treatment. All other colors are subsidiary to or refinements of the principles used in applying red or blue.
3. Color can be introduced into the body from without-in or from within-out by
   a) food;
   b) solarized liquids and solids;
   c) respiration—through color breathing or through projecting sunlight or "artificial" light into the physical and etheric body;
   d) sunlight or "artificial" rays applied to the skin;
   e) meditation on and in color;
   f) color breathing to change the consciousness of the individual and thus to reach the "aura" or the electromagnetic field-force, the cause of the inharmony, and to return the body to physical and emotional health.

Remember: Treat illness on the specific plane of vibration in which it manifests itself. Inward healing from within-out is more effective than outward healing because the inward is derived from awakening the consciousness to color. Chronic disorders progress from without-in, from surface issue toward the vital organ. Cure takes the opposite direction and progresses from within-out and from cephalic to caudal. If the most recent illness is the first to go and those that antedated them are the next to go in reverse order, then all is well.

Here Hering's Law of Healing applies. If the patient shows symptoms of the former disease, this is a normal reaction. In illness, **the disease,** the controlling factor brings on crisis at the specific time for that illness whether or not the organism is ready. If the body can withstand the crisis, it lives even if it has to sacrifice a part or parts in doing so. In the process of curing itself, **the body** is strong enough to bring on a crisis of short duration for that disease and to overcome all symptoms and sub-clinical manifestations without damage to the body.

4. Recall the various properties of color and apply them at the strategic moment in the proper way.
5. Various colors affect the different systems in the body in different ways. The stronger the color, the greater is its effect. The blue part of the spectrum soothes and relaxes. The red part of the spectrum stimulates, activates, and irritates.
6. The purer the color, the more penetrating the rays and the faster the reaction.
7. Do not overload one system at the expense of another. Remember: When treating infections, fevers, and toxin-producing illnesses, that the circulatory system bears the major brunt of eliminating these poisons and should not be overlooked.
8. A good rule to follow: when in doubt, undertreat; do not overtreat.
9. Over-exposure is rarely serious in colortherapy, as it is in chemotherapy where an over-exposure or over-dose to a drug that is poisonous always has serious consequences and may result in death. Over-exposure of one color is remedied, as a general rule by treating with the complementary color.
10. Wrong use of color can be serious. Do not confuse the wrong use of color with over-exposure. As a general rule, if wrong color has been used, first treat with the complementary color to the wrong color; then treat the condition itself.
11. Length of exposure differs for every individual and for each disease and with the type color-medium used. It is always better to under-expose than to over-expose.

The following must be taken into consideration.

a) climate
b) weather
c) quality of filter
d) time of day and season
e) nature of disease
f) sensitivity of patient
g) color
h) bio-rhythm
i) color medium
   (see principle 12)

Some colors require a longer exposure than others. The red end of the spectrum has a quicker visible effect on the skin than the blue, but requires longer exposure. The red rays of the spectrum draw the blood to the surface and redden the skin. The blue rays (chemical and electrical) send the blood inward, reduce heat, and ease pain in inflamed conditions. The blue rays are usually faster acting than the red rays which have a heating and stimulating action.

12. The healing powers of the different colors in glass, in filters, and in dyes are different from the natural colors. Red, for instance, is the hottest visible color, but red glass does not transmit as much heat as orange or yellow glass. It is the power to transmit color, not the visual effect, that is important in this case.

13. The converse of this principle is to be considered. If color is misapplied or misused, it can destroy.
    a) The eye can be shocked by color as the ear, to sound.
    b) Poor color schemes will lead to fatigue.
    c) Too strong colors often irritate.
       Red, yellow and orange fatigue and irritate sooner than the other colors. They are heat-producing and exciting. A red room will raise the blood pressure; but a green room will lower the blood pressure.
    d) Different color effects are to be remembered in healing.
       1) Blue and green are soothing and cooling.
       2) Red against white develops a blue-green reaction.
       3) Blue-green against white develops a red reaction.
       4) Violet against white develops a blue reaction.
       5) Yellow against white develops a blue reaction.

6) Green against white develops a violet reaction.
7) Red stimulates: blue soothes: for example, red pajamas should not be used for sleeping since the color stimulates and raises the blood pressure. A blue lamp alongside the bed will induce sleep.
14. No two individuals react the same way to color. Some respond faster than others:
   a) One may respond better to blue and another to indigo.
   b) If blue is to be used for an inflammatory condition, the pulse, tension, and blood pressure are to be considered. A light blue is indicated if the pulse tension and blood pressure are high; deep blue, if they are low.
   c) The opposite applies to green, which lowers blood pressure.
15. The absorption by the skin of color rays affects all glands, all blood cells, and all chemical and physical conditions of the body. The vital organs have direct connections with the skin through the arterioles, veins, capillaries, and nervous system.
16. The application of light rays in or to one spot of the body affects the entire blood stream through the circulation and elimination of toxins. (The converse of this rule confronts most healers. Selye calls this condition stress. Speransky says a mild stimulus over a long period of time kills. Here the example is cited of the dangers in hair dyes, powders, etc.)
17. Any process, light, or heat, that draws blood to the surface thus relieves congestion of the liver, spleen, kidneys, lungs, gastro-intestinal tract and spinal cord.
18. Light rays
   a) dilate or contract the blood vessels;
   b) elevate or lower blood pressure;
   c) increase the red blood cells;
   d) stimulate the movement of the white blood corpuscles;
   e) aid the leucocytes to destroy bacteria and
   f) confer natural immunity against disease;
   g) assist the tissues in destroying parasites;
   h) increase the activity of the mucous membranes;

i)   increase the oxidizing power of the blood;

j)   regulate collagen between tissue and bone.

19. The color of the clothing worn and the colors in the hair-dyes, lotions, etc., affect the body.

In the matter of clothing, white transmits more of the light rays than does dark clothing, and the light rays have a more animating effect on the body. Red can be worn when it is desired to warm any part of the body; for cold feet, red tissue paper placed inside the socks or red socks will have a more warming effect than a hot water bottle. A blue or lilac undergarment will reflect the cool electrical rays and calm the individual when one deals with an overheated or excited system.

Different colored clothing should be worn and a color change experienced every day of the week so that the color vibrations are not disturbed, but working in harmony. One should avoid the widow's pattern of dress that is seen so frequently in Mexico. These women who wear black develop a "black mentality" or "blackitis", and they all become dejected as a result of the color vibrations. The Chinese were very perceptive when they decreed the mourning color to be white. Men especially in Western society should watch the color of their suits, for they tend to be monochromatic in dress, and these vibrations affect their health.

In the matter of dyes, Dr. Gerson, treating cancer patients, reported that hair dyes have caused cancer and have even caused the disease to flare up in arrested cases.

20. "Artificial" light (an incandescent bulb) and natural light are color vibrations that heal by stimulation, oxidation of toxins, and vitalization—all ancillary to nature which heals.

21. Color healing aims to re-establish color balance and to release tension caused by color starvation that comes from errors in thinking, feeling, nutrition, posture, and other aspects of wrong living habits. Color healing brings about a renewal of life forces in all parts of man's being.

22. Color therapy can be given at a distance successfully if the healer can hit the target—the patient. This principle is used in

the physical world in guided missiles, radionics, radio, and television.

23. Color therapy can be given to oneself by following the same principles used in healing others.

24. Trigger-points are the areas that affect the body drastically: like an atomic explosion. Some of these trigger-points are more powerful than others and react rapidly and sometimes even dramatically.

This factor must be accounted for in colortherapy, as any other therapy.

Watch:

a) The Endocrine Glands, also known as the chakras. Check especially the Pituitary as the master gland of the body and treat this carefully since it controls all other glands

b) The Occipital-Atlantoid Area

c) The Carotids

d) The Fontanels—the Anterior is slower in reaction than is the Posterior

e) The Gluteals

The author presents below only a partial list of the colors normally associated with the various parts of the healthy body. Further, he wishes to remind the healer to apply principles, not to become a push button therapist or a color chart reader. The direct application of color principles will be itemized in the following chapter where the color treatments are suggested for the diseases.

Normal Colors for Healthy Body Parts

Arteries—light red

Bowels—yellow with greenish red

Brain—red and all warm colors

Feet—red and all warm colors

Head—blue and all cool colors

Heart—dark red

Lungs—orange, red, some yellow

Medulla Oblongata—dark red

Glands
   Adrenal—bright purple
   Pineal—blue lavender
   Pituitary—blue, yellow
   Thymus—gold, pink
   Thyroid–green, gold

merging to bluish white
  at the spine
Veins—blue

Clairvoyants' View of Organs of Body and Color Treatment

Scientists have begun to work with those gifted individuals who have "extra-sensory sight" and to test the color descriptions of the body that these people have seen. For this reason, the colors of the body parts and the various vibrations as described by the clairvoyants are enumerated. They see these colors associated with the following parts of the body; and in treatment, one should use the complementary colors: e.g., the complementary color for the bone (which is seen by the clairvoyant as green) is red, and red should be used in treatment.

TABLE 1

Organ	Color Seen	Treat With
Brain centers	yellow-violet	indigo
Bone	green	red
Cerebrospinal system	yellow	violet
Circulatory system	blue	red
Glandular system	violet	yellow or orange
Heart	orange	violet
Kidney	indigo	red
Lungs	yellow	violet
Muscular system	red	green
Skin	indigo	red
Sympathetic system with heart	orange	violet
Sympathetic system as a whole	sea green	red

Trigger Points and Selecting Areas in Treating Organs of the Body with Their Respective Colors

Another list of color treatment is herein also provided to stress the fact that the practitioner practices an art and its principles; he is the artist, not the artisan who uses push-button techniques. He must always consider the patient, the type of imbalance, the system or systems involved, and then use the consequent colors these factors dictate for the restoration of balance and harmony.

1. The nerve centers, particularly those in the spine and the solar plexus, are the most important points of treatment.
2. Next in importance are the forehead, the back of the neck, the chest, and the abdomen. The general policy is to strengthen the entire system, but in some cases local applications are indicated. The color the individual lacks is the one that should be applied. If there is an overabundance of a particular color, neutralize it with a complementary color.
3. Trigger points are areas that affect the body drastically. There are five major areas: the Endocrine Glands (or chakras), the Fontanels, the Occipital-Atlantoid area, the Carotids, and the Gluteals.

Color and Areas to Be Used in Treating the Following Organs and Systems

Brain—Treat the area of scalp, face, back of neck and feet. Treat with soothing indigo, blue, or violet to quiet the blood and nerves.

Heart—Treat that part of the chest over the heart and then the feet and arms. Use soothing indigo, blue or violet to quiet the blood and nerves. Use orange to stimulate the blood and nerves.

Cerebro-Spinal System—Treat the right side of the brain with yellow and violet.

Circulatory System and its Organs—To soothe, use dark green; to invigorate use grass green; to stimulate, use bright red. Note that blue can be substituted for green if there is no hypertension.

Face—Treat the back of the neck. Color depends on the nature of the disease.

Extremities—Treat the arms or legs with red; except in cases of shock.

Glands—See Chakras, in Chapter 2 for areas. The ductless glands contain secretions for harmonizing every body function. Any deviation from the normal color of the gland will show malfunctioning. Treat with green. To activate the glands, use yellow first and then blue.

Hypochrondium—Areas to be treated are lower back, loins, groins, hips, feet, the entire abdominal area—especially the navel region. Treat with the red rays of the spectrum: red, orange, and yellow are to stimulate the gastric juices, the blood, nerves, and peristaltic action of the gastro-intestinal tract.

Use the blue end of the spectrum: blue violet and indigo for diarrhea and inflammation.

Treat the epigastrium with blue for psychological disturbances.

Hypogastrium and Loins—Areas to be treated same as Hypochrondrium. Treat with green for tonic effect; with yellow for stimulating the nerves; with blue for relaxing the muscles.

Kidneys and Renal Parts—Areas to be treated are the lower back, the groins, loins, hips, and feet. Treat with yellow.

Lungs—Area to be treated is the middle of the sternum on line with the second rib. Treat with yellow and violet.

Muscular System—Treat left side of the head with red.

Neck and thorax—Treat with purple on local areas.

Nervous System—Areas to be treated: the right and left sides of the brain. Use violet and lavender to soothe; grass green to invigorate; medium yellow and orange to inspire.

Skin—Treat locally with yellow.

Solar Plexus—Treat the area with the color of the spectrum that the condition dictates.

Sexual Organs—Ovaries and uterus, testes and prostate—treat as indicated in areas listed for kidney; color depends on condition.

Rectum—Treat area as listed for kidney; color is determined by condition.

Nota Bene: Always treat any and all chronic conditions with lemon.

Apparatus and General Directives Applying to All Color Treatments

1. **Construction of Lamp and Color Slides; Choice of Bulbs**
   a) **Choice of Bulb**—The bulb should be about three hundred watts in strength for best results. If color slides are not used, then different colored bulbs would have to be obtained to include the seven colors of the spectrum as well as lemon. Turquoise, magenta, scarlet and purple. **Do not use an ultra-violet bulb.**
   b) **Slides: Their Uses in Combination**—Before the lamp is selected or constructed, be sure to obtain a set of color slides if colored bulbs are not used. Five clear slides, plastic or glass, should be selected: red, yellow, green, violet, and blue. The other two spectrum colors are obtained by combining slides:
      1) Red and yellow give orange.
      2) Blue and violet give indigo.
      3) Yellow and green give lemon.
      4) Green and blue give turquoise.
      5) Red and violet give magenta.
      6) Violet gives a low luminosity. Try to obtain a separate slide of magenta.
      7) Magenta and red give scarlet.
      8) Blue and red give scarlet.

9) Magenta and violet give purple.

10) Yellow and violet give purple.

c) **Filter Paper**—May be used in place of glass slides. Be sure not to allow the paper to be destroyed.

d) **Construction of Lamp**
1. The lamp should be constructed so that it can accommodate to the easy manipulation of inserting the slides or colored bulbs with ease and without burning the operator or the patient. There should be some mode of ventilation. Further, the lamp should be mounted on a stand that can be tilted to various angles and raised or lowered without difficulty.
2. The housing for the bulb or colored glass should be constructed in such a manner that all the light is reflected **to the front** and emerges from the lamp only through the opening covered by the slides or the bulb in use. The light reaching the patient should be filtered by the colored slide covering the white bulb or be directly reflected by the colored bulb.
3. Provision should be made for inserting and changing the colored slides or bulbs without difficulty. The apparatus should be properly ventilated so that no appreciable amount of heat is felt by the patient. The object is to treat the patient, not to burn him. The goal is **light, not heat.**

2. **Exposure to Light: Rules**

For colors on the hot side of the spectrum—red, orange, and yellow—expose for three to ten minutes. In acute cases, longer exposure can be used.

For colors on the cold side of the spectrum—blue, indigo, violet—expose for fifteen to thirty minutes except for cases of high fever, severe burns, and infections or severe pain. In such cases an hour or longer of exposure is indicated.

3. **Treatment with Color: Rules**

In ordinary cases, treatment should be given once or twice

a day. In acute or severe cases, treatment should be more often.

Color should be directed on the bare skin. All other parts should be covered.

Do not overtreat. Undertreat if in doubt.

Techniques of Treatment

1. Solarized water
2. Diet
3. Creativity—psychological devices
4. Contrasting color-decor and Creativity
5. Room decor and color
6. Visualization and meditation
7. Color breathing
8. Gem therapy
9. Metals

1. Technique of Solarized Water

Solarized water is water that has been **directly exposed** to the sun for at least an hour in a glass container of a particular color and that has therefore become irradiated. A red vessel will give red solarized water; a blue vessel, blue solarized water. The longer the water remains exposed to the sun, the stronger is its potency. Solarization depends on temperature, geographical location and the same time of day. Philip M. Chancellor suggest this fitting capsule: "Place an ice cube in the glass of water to be solarized. When the ice cube has melted upon exposure to the sun, the water is charged." Imagine an ice cube melting under the sun's rays in India and in the North Pole. It will take less time in India than in the North.

Since blue is antiseptic, it prevents the water from spoiling and can be kept a week or ten days in hot or cold weather. But red, yellow, and orange should be changed every two days in warm weather and every ten days to two weeks in cold weather. Take the necessary precautions to prevent the freezing and breaking of the container. A caution: solarized water should always be sipped.

An illuminating explanation of the action is provided by Franz Bardon who remarked:

"The watery element rules magnetism or the attractive force . . . . Not only water, but every kind of liquid has the specific property of attracting, and according to the contraction, holding fast, no matter whether good or bad influences be concerned. Therefore we may consider the watery element, especially the material kind of it, as an accumulator. The colder the water is, the greater its accumulative capacity. With its full specific weight, namely at 39°F. (above zero); it is most responsive. This notion is not so decisive, for the difference of receptivity of water (or other liquids) up to 43°F. (above zero) is so insignificant and so faintly visible that only a thoroughly trained magician can recognize these differences. If by increasing the heat, water grows lukewarm, its receptivity is rapidly diminishing. Between 97°-99°F. it becomes neutral to magnetism. . . . For instance it is quite impossible to magnetize a dish of hot soup, because the accumulating power of the watery element, by the expansion of the heat present in the water, is balanced or increased if it rises above 99°F.

2. Technique of Diet

Diet should always be the foundation upon which all the other techniques rest. The therapist must consider food and the color equivalents, as the last chapter of this section indicates. Foods of the proper color as dictated by the individual's needs must be recommended for food is nothing more than color materialized by the plant.

3. Technique of Creativity: Psychological Devices

The inner effort of the self to hold itself erect in its environment is the first step in healing. Painting and color can be most useful first as curative and later as effective habits, for the individual begins to awaken to the beauty around him. In cultivating permissiveness, he becomes field-oriented instead of egocentric, so claim the psychologists. Occultly speaking, the response of the soul to color is a renewal in the joy of living. In learning the aesthetic laws of painting, color, harmony, balance, and rhythm, the individual learns balance in himself, said Steiner. When he creates out of color, he discovers his own inner creativity along with his own power of imagination. The innate forces begin to unfold; and this self-discovery constitutes part of his cure. Thus color exercise is an excellent remedy for the emotions.

Have the patient use water colors freely on the paper without any thought of form or object. Let him merely experience the mood and movement of color. The reader is reminded how psychologists especially the Jungians diagnose the mental illness of a patient by his paintings. The colors he uses and the forms he draws are indications of his mental and emotional health. The Rorshach ink blots are designed to bring out color response, and Rorshach red has even become a significant term in our culture.

The spiritual scientist would say this activity brings one into closer attunement with the soul, which lives in color. Unfortunately, most Western religions condition the individual with the negative attitude that disease and suffering are necessary parts of life. The acceptance of this attitude inhibits the individual, and his wrong thinking results in disharmony. The patient could be instructed to meditate on color and to direct his subconscious mind with the idea of health before he goes to sleep. Auto-hypnosis and auto-suggestion become powerful devices.

4. Technique of Contrasting Colors—Combined with Decor and Creativity

Contrast of color is an effective treatment of eye-conditions:

a) A rhythmic treatment of red and blue alternately will benefit short-sightedness and far-sightedness.
b) Blue is helpful in myopia or near-sightedness as it draws the vision outward, deflates the ego, and makes the individual field-oriented.
c) Red rays are used in presbyopia or far-sightedness; the red rays draw the individual back into himself and expand the ego for this individual is too field-oriented.

Spastic and retarded children need color in room decoration:

a) Spastic children have been helped by color treatment and music. Color shadows are shown on a screen in a room appropriately colored and with a background of strong music.
b) Retarded children learn faster in a yellow colored room.

5. Technique of Room Decor and Color Breathing

Another technique is to have the patient in a room decorated entirely in one color. To speed up the process have him sit there, meditate, and do his color breathing. The patient can concentrate on the color mentally and use it in breathing. This is a very effective method to change the electro-magnetic forces from imbalance to harmony.

6. Technique of Visualization and Meditation: Projected by Healer and/or patient

One technique is to have the healer visualize mentally the feelings and thoughts to be transmitted to the patient and then picture vividly the exact color which corresponds to these thoughts and feelings. The vibrations of the healer affect the vibrations of the patient's physical and mental bodies which in turn, affect the "aura" or the electro-magnetic field force.

There seems to be an electrical circuit from the healer to the patient, and a similar color vibration is set up in the patient, a vibration that affects his mental body. At the same time, the color vibrations in the healer's aura set up a similar vibration in the patient's aura and this changes the vibrations from abnormal to normal. This reaction from mind to aura and from aura to mind has powerful healing properties if done correctly. In some cases, cures have been instantaneous, as has been demonstrated by Phineas Quimby, Religious Science, Christian Science, and the New Thought Movement.

What will be said now may shock some physicians: Color therapy can be given at a distance successfully if the healer can hit the target—his patient. This principle is used in the physical world in guided missiles, radio, radionics, and television.

Another technique is have the patient apply to himself the same principles used by the healer in healing others. The patient heals himself or treats himself by his own mental vibrations, and he changes his own wave lengths through the technique of visualization and meditation. One who is accustomed to meditation can flood any weak organ with the color indicated for normalizing that organ if he projects that color in his mind before and during his meditation.

7. Technique of Color-Breathing

The individual should breathe rhythmically from twelve to eighteen times a minute. If possible, he should use the color of the spectrum or its nearest equivalent. Imagine the self engulfed by a white light that enters through the head from the cosmos down to the extremities and floods the entire organism from within and from without. Keep this image for two minutes. Then project the particular color needed by the condition.

Red, yellow and orange, whichever one is used, is visualized as being drawn up from the earth through the soles of the feet to the various organs. The length of time for visualizing the red part of the spectrum is two minutes. This is the force the Hindus call Kundalini.

Blue, violet, and indigo should be visualized as coming down from the atmosphere as vertical rays into the anterior fontanel to the various organs. The length of time for visualizing colors in the blue part of the spectrum is three to four minutes. The Hindus call this force prahna.

Green should be visualized as coming into the navel on the horizontal plane. The length of time for visualizing the color green is one minute in a waving motion upward from the umbilical cord and one minute downward from the umbilical cord, but always on a horizontal plane.

Then mentally bathe the body and allow the entire self to be engulfed in a white light for two minutes.

Remember: White light begins and ends the treatment. For those who know how to concentrate, the few minutes are adequate. But for those whose thoughts wander and who have not mastered the art of meditation, an hour's thought on the requisite color would not be long enough for therapy.

8. Technique of Gem Therapy

Gems are used by some healers in colortherapy because,

a) They are purer in color.
b) They are of one color and are unmixed and unadulterated in effects.
c) The rays are concentrated in the gem.
d) The theory accounting for their use—among the Hindus, Egyptians, and in the East—is that the planets influence human behaviour physically, psychologically, emotionally, and spiritually. Since the gems have the same rays as do the planets, they represent the same influence as the planets do, but not as forcefully.
e) The true color of the gem is revealed by the use of the prism: for example, the rays of a diamond are seen as white by the naked eye, but are indigo when seen under the prism. Therefore indigo is the color of the diamond. A table is given below of the gems, the planets, and the rays used in therapy. It must be noted that all gems and all metals can be used, but those listed in the table furnish very satisfactory results. Further it must be reported that in astrology, all invisible rays are given the generic names of **Rahu** or **Dragon's Head** (shortwave, ultra-violet rays) and **Ketu** or **Dragon's Tail** (longwave, infra-red rays).

GEMS	PLANET	RAY
Ruby	Sun	Red
Pearl	Moon	Orange
Coral	Mars	Yellow
Emerald	Mercury	Green
Moonstone	Jupiter	Blue
Diamond	Venus	Indigo
Sardonyx	**Rahu**	Ultra-violet
Cats Eye	**Ketu**	Infra-red

The term **Roygbiv** is used in physics, but some Indians reverse the term to label these seven rays as **Vibgyor.** Reading it forwards or backwards is of no consequence; this is a matter of cultural labels. What is significant is that the term is interpreted as possessing two properties: static and dynamic. In the static form, the gem can be applied locally: that is, directly on the patient. In another static form, gems of a particular ray may be placed in water, alcohol, or oil and kept there for seven days. When the gem is removed, the procedure is for one drop of the gem-possessed fluid (alcohol; etc.) to be mixed with water or milk to make a mixture that becomes a powerful medicine (homeopathy) which is able to cure the disease for that ray. In the dynamic form, the healer heals from a distance and directs his target or charges it with the proper color.

The gem technique can be applied by having the individual wear gems as rings or ornaments to form a magnetic circle about the person, to guard him against evil, and to restore harmony; by mixing the gems to make the properly irradiated drinks; and by rotating the gems on a disc pointing to a photograph, as has been explained in another section of this study in reference to a technique used by an Indian doctor. To bring the past and the present together one may mention that the Indians, the Chinese and the Egyptians would burn gems and then sell the ashes as medicine. To this day in India, the ashes of the specific gems are available in the market place for any one to buy. They are known by the name of **Bhasmas,** and they are used for the following illnesses.

a) Ruby Ash—tuberculosis, colic, boils, ulcers, pains, liver trouble, eye trouble, constipation, burning sensation in the lower extremities, heart diseases, fevers, emotional illnesses.

b) Pearl Ash—coughs, fever, heart palpitation, complexion, indigestion, mental illness, diabetes, frigidity, impotency, jaundice, alcoholism, tuberculosis.

c) Coral Ash—Liver troubles, parasites, ulcers, blood diseases, venereal diseases, febrile diseases, leprosy, asthma, jaundice, urinary diseases, obesity.

d) Emerald Ash—sterility, stammering, emaciation, loss of appetite, dumbness, deafness, kleptomania, digestive disorders, leucoderma, colic, asthma, piles, ulcers, swelling, debility.

e) Moonstone Ash—paralysis, apoplexy, tumors, emotional disturbances, piles, leprosy, indigestion.

f) Diamond Ash—leprosy, tuberculosis, emaciation, delusion, dropsy, diabetes, fistula, obesity, swellings, sterility, venereal diseases, diabetes.

g) Sapphire Ash—deafness, enlarged spleen, paralysis, dropsy, nervous diseases, emotional diseases.

9. Technique of Treatment with Metals

Some colortherapists use metal instead of gems, but no attempt is made to cover this phase of treatment at this time.

CHAPTER VIII

TREATMENT OF SPECIFIC DISEASES
WITH COLOR

The listing of the diseases and the colors to be used are self-explanatory. But the author has devised this key in referring to the seven chakras and their anatomical equivalents together with the colors of the spectrum:

C 1 signifies the Muladhara Chakra or sacral plexus.
C 2 signifies the Swadhishatana Chakra or prostatic plexus.
C 3 signifies the Manipura Chakra or solar plexus.
C 4 signifies the Anahata Chakra or cardiac plexus.
C 5 signifies the Vishuda Chakra or laryngeal plexus.
C 6 signifies Ajna Chakra or cavernous plexus.
C 7 signifies Sahasrara Chakra or pituitary-cerebral cortex.

The reader who wishes to remind himself of the detailed information about the Chakras should review that section in the chapter on **Views of the Past** with its discussion of the contributions made by Indian thought. The traditional references for color remain as dictated by their spectrum relationship: ROYGBIV-R for red; O for orange; etc.

The listing of the specific diseases concludes with the Chakra reference and the color to be used in treating that Chakra: for example C 3 O should be interpreted to read: Treat Chakra Manipura or the solar plexus with the color orange at that anatomical point identified with the plexus.

One further caution: Remember these two rules about color interchange;

1. Red, orange, yellow can be used interchangeably as can blue, indigo, and violet: TWO SETS OF TRIADS.
2. Green can be used where blue is beneficial; in that respect, blue and green are interchangeable.

Diseases and Their Color Treatment

Alcoholism—treat the area around the navel with red for ten minutes and the forehead with blue for fifteen minutes once daily in acute cases; switch to lemon in chronic cases. C 4 V

Amatrophic Lateral Sclerosis—treat the nervous system with blue for fifteen minutes in acute cases; treat the extremities with lemon for ten minutes and then follow with treatment of nervous system with blue for chronic cases twice daily. C 5 I; C 7 G

Amenorrhea—treat with blue ten minutes each on sacrum, on lower part of abdomen right and left side, and thyroid; treat only twice a week C 1 B

Anemia—treat with red light bath for ten minutes a day, concentrating on the upper dorsals for five minutes; glass of red solarized water daily. C 3 R

Angina Pectoris—see heart.

Angina and Pseudo Angina—see heart.

Anorhexia—treat with blue over umbilical cord for ten minutes.

Aortitis—see heart.

Aphonia—treat with indigo light on the throat for five minutes; repeat every four hours; drink half glass of blue solarized water every two hours and gargle with the other half. C 6 B

Apoplexy—treat with blue over the forehead right over the frontal protuberances. C 7 G

Appendicitis—treat with blue or green on poupart ligament for twenty minutes; same for pseudo. C 3 B

Arm drop—treat lymphatics under the arm with yellow for ten minutes; follow with blue for ten minutes. C 5 V

Arthritis—Articula-treat neck; Gonorrheal-treat the spine; Rheumatoid-see Gonorrhea. C 3 R

Asthma—in adults, red, yellow, or orange can be used. If the system is emaciated, use red one day and yellow the following day. After an attack, use orange. Solarized water is always indicated. In acute stage Indigo or violet is mandatory. Treat for fifteen minutes on chest and upper back. C 3 R

Asthma-Cardiac—treat with red for ten minutes on abdomen.

Asthma-in children—use red on pancreas.

Autointoxication—treat bowels.

Back, general, spinal ache and soreness, same as back pain.

Back Pain—treat as bowels and as gall bladder; use green on small and lower back. C 1 B

Baldness—treat with blue on scalp, fifteen minutes daily. C 4 V

Bells Palsy—see facial paralysis.

Bile, concentrated—see liver and gall bladder. C 6 B

Biliousness—see liver. C 6 B

Bladder—treat with blue, alternate with yellow over the lower spine for ten minutes; a glass of solarized blue water; for incontinence, use green or purple light. C 4 V

Bleeding—see nose ailments; hemorrhage. C 7 G

Blindness—where there is no organic damage, use green for thirty minutes twice daily or violet for twenty minutes twice daily, over fifth dorsal vertebra. C 5 I

Blood Ailments—treat with red. C 3 R

Blood Pressure—see heart.

Boils, Abscesses and Carbuncles—treat with lemon on abdomen just over the navel and three inches on either side of the midline for one minute; treat with orange locally for twenty minutes. When suppuration or throbbing is felt, use yellow until the area bursts open. Remove core. Then use green until pus is drained and a clear red cavity is left. Use Turquoise a few times locally and seal with indigo locally. C 7 G

Bowels—For constipation, use yellow for ten minutes; for diarrhea, use blue or green. A glass of solarized water a day is indicated until the condition is under control. Diet should be looked into.

Brachial Neuritis—See Neuritis C 4 V

Breast—lump in or lymphatic lumps—use green or blue over the fontanels and pancreas. See cancer and mastitis. C 7 G

Bright Disease—See Kidneys. C 5 I

Bronchitis or pneumonia—in acute case, treat with indigo, solarized water, and light; in chronic cases, use red or orange water and light. Treat upper chest on sternum for ten minutes. C 6 B

Bruises—treat locally with magenta C 7 G

Bubonic Plague—treat with blue for fifteen minutes each on back and front four times daily. C 6 B

Burns—Two types: a) From heat; vibrations slower than visible light (below the red spectrum). b) Burns caused by use of Radium, X-ray, frostbites come from vibrations faster than visible light (above the violet end of the spectrum). The vibratory rate or frequency of oscillation of the energy responsible for the burn is the key to the color needed for treatment. Burns caused by excessive heat or hot energy—use blue light to relieve pain. When pain is gone, switch to turquoise to rebuild the skin. Cover the skin with a very thin layer of coconut oil for faster results. Burns caused by excessive cold or cold burn—use the red ray which supplies the deficiency of hot energy that is needed by the body. The last is a good example in healing of the use of color in healing by the injection of the deficient vibratory energies. C 7 G

Cancer—alternate use of indigo and green or orange, using one color one day and the other color the next. Treat the spine for ten minutes. Treat the pituitary, thyroid, adrenal cortex, ovaries or prostate, for five minutes each in that order. Treat abdomen just over navel and three inches of either side of the midline for five minutes. Treat pancreas for five minutes. Finish with light on forehead and temples for five minutes each. C 7 G

Cardiac Conditions or Heart—see heart.

Cataracts—treat with indigo ray over the affected eye for ten minutes; treat bowels. C 5 I

Cerebral—Spinal Meningitis—treat with violet over the spine for twenty minutes. C 7 G

Character Changes—see emotional disorders.

Chicken Pox—treat with ultra-violet on torso for thirty minutes on each side. C 7 G

Cholorsis—See anemia. C 3 R

Chorea or St. Vitus Dance—treat with blue light on front and back for thirty minutes daily for about sixty days; should show excellent results.

Cholera—Treat with violet on abdomen thirty minutes twice daily. C 7 G

Circulation—see heart.

Cirrhosis—see liver.

Claudication, intermittent—treat with blue for twenty minutes over affected area.

Cold—treat with red if no fever is present; use orange if patient suffers from hypertension. Green on head and blue on chest if fever or inflammation is present. C 3 R

Colic—see digestive ailments. C 1 Y

Colitis—see bowels; treat forehead and temples with blue light for three minutes each. C 1 Y

Concussion—treat with violet over the head for twenty minutes. C 7 G

Constipation—see bowels. C 1 Y

Coughs—for dry cough, treat with indigo, solarized water, and light on Chest for ten minutes. For wet cough, substitute orange light and orange solarized water. C 6 B

Convulsions—treat with blue over the occipital area and the spinal cord. Ten minutes on occipital and twenty on spinal cord. C 7 G

Cramps—treat cause. C 7 G

Croup—see lungs. C 5 I

Cystitis—acute chronic see bladder.

Cysts—see cancer. C 7 G

Dandruff—treat with indigo on scalp for ten minutes. C 5 I

Deafness—treat with indigo light on top of the head for five minutes; use indigo on occipital-atlantoid area for ten minutes. Indigo on fifth dorsal for five minutes. Solarized water should be taken twice weekly. If emotional in origin also treat emotions. C 5 I

Debility—treat with orange on forehead. C 4 V

Dehydration—see liquid stools. Treat with blue. C 7 G

Delirium Tremors—see alcoholism. C 4 V

Delusion—see emotional illness. C 5 I

Depression—see emotional illness. C 1 Y

Diabetes—According to Ghadiali, excess sugar in the urine merely indicates glycosuria and does not necessarily indicate diabetes which is an ailment in which there is an excess of sugar in the blood. The body needs carbohydrates and is definitely harmed by carbohydrate starvation (fructose recommended in the diet). Lung action depends on the functioning of the thyroid gland. Orange activates the thyroid which is representative of carbohydrates (the mixture of hydrogen red and carbon yellow). Deprivation of carbohydrates drains thyroid energy, lowers lung activity and blood circulation. Metabolism and nutrition suffer. Milk sugar, galactose, grape sugar, dextrose and fruit sugar, levulose—all have the empirical formula $C_6H_{12}O_6$, but there is a vital difference between the character of the dextrose and levulose in relationship to polarized light. Galactose and dextrose are dextro-rotated; that is they twist the plane of polarized light to the right. Levulose is levo-rotatory: it twists the plane of polarized light to the left. The sugar not assimilated is the dextrose. The levulose is consumed within the tissues and should be included in the diabetic's diet to prevent carbohydrate starvation. The basic cause of Diabetes is a sluggish lympathic system. Lymph plays a large part in assimilation and nutrition. Since it is a chronic disorder, the color indicated is lemon followed by yellow (lymphatic activator). Lemon for fifteen minutes over the solar plexus followed by yellow; then treat as liver. C 5 I

Diarrhea—treat with blue light over abdomen for thirty minutes, Solarized water-one glass daily. C 7 G

Digestive Ailments—treat with yellow on abdomen and yellow solarized water except for inflammations and diarrhea. C 3 R   Colic—C1Y;   Dyspepsia—C1Y;   Hyper-acidity—C7G; Hypoacidity—C7G; Indigestion—C1Y; Stomach troubles—C1Y.

Diphtheria—treat with blue light over the solar plexus, throat and back of neck for thirty minutes every four hours. C 7 G

Diverticulitis—see bowels.

Dysentery—treat with blue light. C 6 B—Amebic, C 5 I; Bacillary C 7 G

Dyspepsia—see digestive ailments. C 1 Y

Dropsy—treat with blue light on affected part. C 6 B

Duodenal Ulcer—treat with blue light on abdominal area for thirty minutes; blue light on forehead and temples for three minutes each. Solarized water—one glass daily. C 7 G

Duodentis—see bowels. C 1 Y

Dysmenorrhea in young women—same as Amenorrhea. C 1 B

Ear Ailments—see Deafness. C 5 I

Eczema—Dry, treat with blue light over affected part for ten minutes; Wet, treat with Magenta; a glass of solarized water daily. C 5 I

Elbow Tenderness—treat Pancreas with blue. C 3 V

Emotional Disorders and illness—treat with blue light over the forehead and the temples for fifteen minutes except in catatonic cases, where orange is substituted for blue. Delusion — C 5 I; Depression — C 1 Y; Eneursis—see bladder; Hallucinations—C 5 I; Insanity—C 2 O; Irritations—C 5 I; Mania—C 7 G; Nervous Exhaustion—C 1 Y

Neuroses—C 4 D; Obsessions—C 5 G

Endo-Carditis and Myo-Carditis—see heart and circulation.

Endocrine glands—treat with red at the base of the spine.

Enuresis—treat as in emotional Disorders; but treat bladder as well. C 4 V

Epilepsy—treat with blue light over the head, spine and solar plexus for twenty minutes. Treat abdomen for five minutes; see convulsions. C 7 G

Erysipelas—treat with red for ten minutes and blue for fifteen minutes. C 7 G

Eye—in inflammation, use blue light for fifteen minutes. For Myopia, use blue light. For presbyopia, use red light; for Strabismus, use yellow and finish with blue. C 5 I

Exopthalamus—Toxic Goiter; treat Muller's Muscle. C 6 B

Facial Paralysis or Bells Palsy—treat with yellow for ten minutes; then with blue for ten minutes. C 3 R

Fevers—treat with blue light front and back, fifteen minutes each. C 7 G

Fistula—treat with blue light for ten minutes. C 5 I

Flatulence—treat with purple light over the abdomen for fifteen minutes; solarized water should be taken every day. C 3 R

Frigidity—treat Coccygeal area with blue for fifteen minutes daily; treat ovaries with orange five minutes on each side. C 1 I

Gall bladder—treat with orange for ten minutes in affected area; see bowels. C 2 O

Gall Stones—treat with orange light on the abdomen about three inches above the navel for fifteen minutes; drink orange solarized water. C 2 O

Gastritis—see gastro-intestinal ailments.

Gastric Ulcer—treat with yellow light over the abdomen and lower back for fifteen minutes each. Apply blue light on forehead and temples for three minutes. C 7 G

Gastro-Intestinal Ailments—treat with yellow light on abdomen and yellow solarized water except for inflammations and diarrhea.

Glaucoma—treat with blue rays over the eyes for thirty minutes. Correct diet. C 1 V

Goiter—treat with blue light on the thyroid for fifteen minutes daily. A glass of solarized water daily. C 6 B

Gonads—treat cause; see gonorrhea; see syphilis. C 1 V

Gonorrhea—treat with blue light over lumbars and genital organs for forty-five minutes daily for two to six weeks. Every three days use green instead of blue. For reinfection; use lemon. C 1 V

Gout—treat with orange over abdomen for ten minutes; and blue over the toes and wrists for fifteen minutes. C 4 V

Granular Lid—see eyes. C 5 I

Gum Boil—see toothache. C 5 I

Hallucination—see emotional illness. C 5 I

Hay Fever—treat with yellow light on abdomen for ten minutes; blue light over the face and chest for twenty minutes. C 7 G

Headaches—Brow, see bowels.

Crown—treat pelvic area.

Lateral right—see liver.

Frontal—see bowels.

Occipital—see bowels.

Temporal—treat over eyebrows with blue for 15 minutes.

Heartburn—see flatulence. C 3 R

Heart-Circulation—treat with red rays to stimulate the heart; C 3 R; treat with blue rays to quiet the heart;

Palpitation—use blue over the heart and red over the solar plexus and yellow over the abdomen. C 6 B

High blood pressure—use light blue or green. C 7 G

Low blood pressure—use red. C 6 B

Angina and hypertrophy—use Magenta—It reinforces the heart action and corresponds with the vibratory rate of Lethiumin, Potassium, Strontium, and Manganese all used in energizing the heart.

Stenosis, Incompetence of heart valve, Cardiac

Dilation and Bradycardia—use scarlet.

For excessive palpitation and for all inflammation; for Myocarditis, Endocarditis, Pericarditis and Aortic Aneurism, use purple. C 7 G

Hemiplegic—treat lumbar area with yellow. See paralysis.

Hemorrhoids—see Piles. C 1 B

Hemorrhage—treat with blue light over the affected area.

Hepatitis—treat with blue light over the fifth rib on the right side in the midline for five minutes. See bowels. C 6 B

Hernia—treat locally with blue in acute cases for fifteen minutes; treat with lemon in chronic cases for twenty minutes for two weeks; then switch to Turquoise. C 3 R

Hiccough—treat with blue and green light on the fifth vertebra for five minutes.

Hoarseness—see aphonia. C 6 5

Hydrophobia—treat with blue light for two to three hours daily; solarized water is indicated. C 7 G

Hyperacidity—see digestive ailments.

Hyperchlorhydria—treat with blue light for twenty minutes on stomach.

Hypermotility—of the G.I. tract—same as above.

Hypertension—see emotional disorders.

Hyperthyroidism—see goiter.

Hypoacidity—see digestive ailments.

Hypochlorhydria—treat with red or orange for twenty minutes on the stomach.

Hypoglycemia—see liver.

Hysteria—treat with blue on forehead for fifteen minutes. C 5 I

Impotency—treat with yellow on small of back for fifteen minutes; then with indigo for fifteen minutes. C 7 B

Indigestion—see digestive ailments. C I Y

Inflammation—all, treat with blue generally and locally. C 7 G

Influenza—see liver. C 7 G

Insanity—see emotional illness. C 2 O

Insomnia—treat with blue light over forehead and temples for five minutes. C 2 O

Intermittent Claudication—treat with blue for twenty minutes over the affected area. C 6 V

Iritis—treat with blue over eyes for thirty minutes. C 7 B

Irritation—see emotional illness. C 5 I

Itching—treat with blue over affected area for ten minutes. C 6 B

Jaundice—see hepatitis. C 6 B

Kidneys—treat with blue light for ten minutes over kidney area; alternate with orange. If chronic, use lemon. C 4 V

Kidney stones—treat with orange light for fifteen minutes and drink solarized water. C 4 O

Knee trouble—see gall bladder, gonorrhea.

Laryngitis—see Aphonia. C 6 B

Leprosy—treat with lemon over the affected parts for thirty minutes twice daily and treat organs involved. C 5 I

Leucoderma—disease of pigmentation—treat with with blue over affected area; in cases of hypertension, change to violet or orange. C 5 I

Leucorrhea—see amenorrhea. C 1 B

Leukemia—see cancer. C 3 R; C 7 G

Liquid Stools—treat with blue for twenty minutes over the abdomen.

Listlessness—treat with red. C 1 R

Liver—see hepatitis.

Local Injuries—treat locally.

Lumbago—treat with yellow light on abdomen for fifteen minutes; treat with blue light on lower lumbars and sacrum for fifteen minutes. C 4 V

Lungs—treat with ultra-violet for ten minutes. C 5 I

Lupus—treat with blue over affected part for thirty minutes; drink solarized water. C 7 G

Malaria—treat with blue during feverish state and yellow during chill. Blue to be used on head area. C 6 B

Malignancies—see cancer. C 7 G

Mania—see emotional illness. C 7 G

Mastitis—treat with blue light on ovaries for five minutes; on breast for ten minutes; from first to sixth dorsal for ten minutes; on forehead and temple for three minutes each. C 1 V

Mastoiditis—treat with blue light over ears and 5th dorsal lumbar; for thirty minutes.

Measles—treat with yellow and red at first and then follow with blue over torso for twenty minutes. C 7 G

Melancholia—treat with red for half an hour. C 3 R

Menier Syndrome—treat bowels and treat head with blue for twenty minutes. C 6 B

Meningitis—see spinal meningitis. C 7 G

Menopause—treat with blue for twenty minutes over ovaries; yellow for ten minutes over kidney; and green for ten minutes over forehead. C 7 G

Menstruation—Cessation—treat with orange for twenty minutes. C 1 B

Mental Disorders—treat with violet.

Mental Exhaustion—treat with orange half an hour.

Migraine—see headache.

Milk Leg—see phlebitis.

Moles—see growths. C 3 R

Mumps—treat with blue light on parotid gland for ten minutes; sexual parts for ten minutes. C 7 G

Myocarditis—see heart circulation.

Nausea—treat with blue for twenty minutes in the abdominal area. C 4 B

Nephritis—see kidney.

Nervous Disorders—treat with green. C 4 V

Nervous Exhaustion—see emotional illness. C 1 Y

Neuralgia—see kidney. C 6 B

Neuritis—Brachia—treat cause whether from kidney, gall bladder, or pancreas. C 4 V

Neuroses—see emotional illness. C 4 V

Nightblindness—see eyes. C 3 R

Nightmare—see emotional disorders. C 1 B

Nose Ailments—Bleeding, treat with indigo until it stops C 7 G; treat other conditions with Indigo. C 5 V

Obsession—see emotional illness. C 5 G

Oralsepsis—treat mouth with violet for fifteen minutes. Solarized water wash indicated. C 7 G

Orchitis—treat with blue over the groin and testicles for thirty minutes. C 1 B

Ovary—treat with blue light for ten minutes. C 1 B

Ovarian cysts—see tumors.

Pain-back—treat cause; see back pain.

Palsy—see Parkinsons. C 5 V

Paralysis—treat with yellow on back of the neck for ten minutes, indigo on spine for ten minutes, indigo on sacrum and coccyx for ten minutes; treat each sciatic nerve with yellow and indigo for twenty minutes. C 3 R

Paralysis-infantile—see acute polomyelitis. C 7 G; C 3 R-chronic.

Paraplegic—see paralysis.

Parkinsons Disease—treat nervous system with blue in acute cases for thirty minutes; follow with violet on top of head near posterior fontanels for fifteen minutes, In chronic cases treat with lemon for fifteen minutes, then follow as above. C 5 I

Paratid Glands—see mumps.

Peritonitis—treat with blue, indigo for twenty minutes. C 7 G

Phlebitis or Milk Leg—treat with blue light on sixth cervicle and affected part for twenty minutes. Chronic, use lemon.

Phlegmatic Fever—see fever. C 5 I

Piles or Hemorrhoids—treat with red light on sixth cervicle for ten minutes; blue light on lower lumbars and sacrum for ten minutes. C 1 Y

Pneumonia—treat with indigo on upper chest for thirty minutes make sure the light hits the sternum on second rib; see bronchitis. C 5 I

Polio-Meyelitis-Acute—treat with indigo for thirty minutes over the spine. Repeat thrice daily. Treat Pancreas. C 7 G

Potts Disease—treat with red light over the front and back for twenty minutes. Follow with blue light for ten minutes. Treat the spinal cord with red and blue light. See tuberculosis. C 7 G

Prostate Condition—treat with indigo over prostate area; then treat bladder. See cancer. C 1 V

Ptosed Eyelid—diet and see bowels.

Pylorus, Spasm—see heart and liver.

Quincy Sore Throat—see throat. C 6 B

Rabies—treat with indigo over the affected parts for thirty minutes and ten minutes on sixth cervical for ten minutes four times daily. C 7 G

Raynauds Disease—treat with red light for twenty minutes on hands and toes. C 6 B

Rectal Spasm—treat with blue.

Rheumatism-Acute—use blue or green solarized water and light on affected parts for thirty minutes. Chronic-substitute lemon or orange. C 4 V

Rickets—treat with ultra-violet on chest for twenty minutes. C 6 B

Round Shoulders in Children—see bowels.

St. Vitus Dance—see chorea.

Scalp—treat with violet over area for fifteen minutes.

Scarlet Fever—same as measles; treat with blue light on spinal cord for forty-five minutes; red at start for five minutes. C 7 G

Sciatica—see lumbago.

Sclerosis-Multiple—treat with indigo at occipital-atlantoid area for thirty minutes. C 7 V

Scurvy—vitamin deficiency; see skin. C 4 B

Shock—treat with blue light on sixth cervical for ten minutes and indigo on upper chest area for twenty minutes. Treat extremities. C 6 B

Sinusitis—see bowels; treat with blue for ten minutes on third dorsal; green on head and blue on sinus. C 7 G

Skin-Internal in origin: Two classifications—1) The moist or weeping type-preponderance of energy from the hot side of the spectrum. 2) Dry scaling disorder due to a preponderance of energy from the cold side of the spectrum. As a general rule, the latter type should be converted to the moist, weeping type before it is likely to heal: Treat: Dry scaly type with green and then switch to lemon. If moist or weeping has not appeared, switch to yellow or orange. For moist or weeping, use gold, then turquoise. If obstinate, change to blue or indigo. Use no alkaline soap. C 1 B

Small-Pox—same as scarlet fever—treat with red light to prevent pox marks. C 7 G

Smell Deficiency—treat with Indigo for fifteen minutes. C 7 G

Solar Plexus—treat with yellow over solar plexus area.

Spasm—treat cause-right shoulder kidney, gall bladder; see bowels. C 6 B

Sphincter, Internal—treat cause.

Spinal Ache—treat cause.

Spinal Meningitis—see polio or acute poliomyelitis. C 7 G

Spleen—treat with yellow over spleen area for half hour. C 3 O

Sterility—treat base of sacrum with indigo for half hour. C 1 B

Stomach Disorder—see digestive ailments. C 1 Y

Stools, Liquid—see liquid stools; see diarrhea.

Strepthroat—see throat. C 7 C

Syphilis—treat with green and blue light over spinal cord and chest for twenty minutes daily for several weeks. Then switch to lemon for several weeks. Solarized water is indicated. C 7 G

Synovities—treat with yellow or red; apply to affected part for ten minutes. C 1 O

Tabes Dorsalis—treat nervous system with blue. C 4 V

Tetanus—treat nervous system with violet for thirty minutes four times daily. C 7 G

Throat—Strep—treat with indigo or blue for twenty minutes. C 7 G

Typhus—treat with blue light over spinal cord for thirty minutes every four hours. C 7 G

Tonsilitis—treat with blue light on throat and back of neck for thirty minutes. C 6 V

Toothache—treat with blue light or solarized water on affected tooth. C 6 B

Torticollis—Wry Neck—see bowels; treat with blue and green for ten minutes at sixth dorsal.

Toxic Diseases—see bowels.

Trifacial Neuralgia—treat kidney on the affected side.

Tuberculosis—treat with orange over chest and back for thirty minutes; then follow with violet for ten minutes. If constipated, use yellow light over abdomen; finish with light over forehead and temples for three minutes each. Orange has both calcium and copper, the two elements needed to repair lung tissue. To stop leakage in the lungs, calcium is needed. Calcium is very important in the maintenance of the lung tissues. Turquoise is specified for use during the period when fever is present. If fever increases, switch to blue. C 7 G

Tumor—breast—see cancer. C 4 V

Typhoid—see bowels; use blue solarized water and light. C 7 G

Ulcer—see duodenal ulcer and gastric ulcer. C 7 G

Urethritis—Post—see gonhorrhea and bladder. C 1 V

Urticaria—see skin. C 7 G

Vaginal Disorders—treat cause.

Vertigo—see deafness. C 7 G

Vomitting—see anorexia.

Vomitting of Pregnancy—treat with indigo or violet for fifteen minutes daily. C 6 B

Whooping Cough—treat with blue or violet on chest and upper back for thirty minutes twice daily, for a week to ten days. C 5 V

Wounds—treat with violet on wound; depends on the extent and severity of the wound, for time will vary from ten minutes to one hour. C 7 G

Yellow fever—treat with blue light on head and yellow light on the abdomen. C 7 G

CHAPTER IX

FOODS AND THEIR COLORS

Man has the same mechanism as the plant for the manufacturing of food. Through his skin and eyes, he absorbs the various colors directly as the plants do and this absorption through the skin and eyes is a form of digestion. At present, this method is an auxiliary to the digestive process if the body does not obtain all the color rays it needs. Since the eyes, as Bergson and Simpson said, need color for food they too also go through a form of digestion. Skin and eyes play a role in digestion.

Man is a predatory animal and a parasite because he has to live off plants and other animals. Without plants, no life could exist in its present form. What the plant does is to take light, which is color, and then through a process of photosynthesis, the plant comes into being: flower, fruit or vegetable. The form is determined—as is its pattern and shape—by its heritage of potential rhythm. All man does by digestion is to take solid matter, now called food, break it down, through the process of digestion, into its ionized state where it can be absorbed by the body and into the body.

What this process of metabolism does is reverse the plant's synthesis, and man takes the light into his cells of the seven cosmic rays of the universe in certain combinations about which scientists know very little and in a scaled range which if adhered to produces harmony and health. Any change in the combinations, any violation or any deviations from the scaled range (too much or too little of light) produce alteration with its consequence: disease. But certain specifics about foods and their colors are known:

1. Red, yellow, and orange are colors which have an alkaline effect, and the foods with these colors have the same effect.

2. Blue, violet, and indigo are colors which have an acid effect, and the foods with these colors have the same effect.
3. Green is a neutral color, and therefore has neither acid nor alkaline effect; green foods are consequently neutral.

The statement that green foods are neither acid nor alkaline is not to be confused with the nutritional aspects of the diet where fruits and vegetables are given for acidosis. The rationale here is that the fruits and vegetables have an alkalizing reaction and thereby neutralize the acid of the proteins.

When the foods and their respective colors are listed, the mere recital of the color rays with their acid, alkaline, or neutral reactions is not quite sufficient. Important too is information about the energy potential, the soil, the geography, the variations in the cosmic rays as a result of changes in climate, season and temperature, and the particular hemisphere in which one is located and in which the food is grown—all of which affect taste.

Science is now coming around to what the Hindus and Chinese have known, what the ancients have announced, and what astrological,[1] charts have used for centuries. These teachings, of what science is inclined to call the "lunatic fringe," are now being reassessed and reconsidered.

Scientists accept the fact that the moon affects the tides and the sun affects the planets. The astrologers say that the position of the planet and its relation to other planets at all times of the year affected each other, as well as the specific individual. Both planets and man come under the influence of cosmic vibrations. As planets go into certain orbital positions with the changes in the seasons the rate of vibration changes.

But one does not have to accept the generalizations of the Hindus or of astrology. One can look to the pattern of process, the seasonal changes, familiar to all. The rhythm of the universe expresses itself annually. The pattern exists, partly seen and partly not, and all explanations that this transformation is due to changes in the weather are merely confirmations.

1. This use of astrology has no relationship to its misuse for purposes of fortune-telling and other mystical nonsense.

In his book **Spirit in Matter**, L. Kolisko reported a series of experiments, the findings of which are of great pertinence here. These experiments suggest that a pattern-forming potential exists capable of having an effect on "dead" mineral matter, and that this pattern changes as the seasons change. So consistent is this pattern-making potential that from impregnated papers it is possible to select the one produced on Easter Sunday, for instance, year after year. Within this particular pattern always occurs a design suggestive of a partly-opened tulip bloom. It is therefore possible to perceive in matter that is usually considered to be quite devoid of life something more than a mere collection of atoms at the mercy only of mechanical forces. Dr. Charles W. Littlefield discovered that if minerals were moistened and the water permitted to evaporate, a vital force appeared in the mineral particles having the characteristics of the various tissues of the body. Drs. H.S. Burr and F.C.S. Northrop of Yale University demonstrated the existence of the electro-dynamic field which they named the electrical architect. Its pattern is always the same: man is born within this field, grows to maturity and then dies in it; this field and pattern of existence contain in themselves all the interacting forces which give direction throughout the life span of the individual. Hence it is easily possible to imagine that some pattern-making potential exists in space. A chemical process repeats itself; nature repeats itself every year. Somewhere in the universe must exist a blue-print that makes repeatability possible.

But what relationship to food and color and consequently to healing has this pattern-making potential? The Hindu theory of vibrations? The Yin and Yang principles of the Chinese? The astrological interpretations of the seasons of the year? The rays that the astrologers and the philosophers describe and the potential that the scientists talk about all are reflected in the foods as those forces of nature (sun, moon, photosynthesis, etc.,) responsible for life and the growth of plants and animals including man. The theories all point in the same direction, but one must stress the basic identity in vibration and color that binds all these appraisals together.

Both the Chinese and the Indian teach that all foods are composed of the seven rays of the spectrum and the five elements. The foods vary in composition and effectiveness because of the difference in the quality and quantity of these seven rays and the five elements. All the foods have taste because of the disintegration of matter. This disintegration is interpreted by the olfactory organs and then is **reflexed** to the tongue which distinguishes the basic six tastes (here the reader is reminded that the Chinese use only five tastes) as follows:

1. Sweet   3. Saline   5. Bitter
2. Sour   4. Pungent   6. Astringent

The Indians believe that the tongue is the convertor or the great signal transformer, but the author asserts that the nose is the radar-signalizer. Whether it be nose or tongue, both play a vital role in the digestive process—especially in the first unit of digestion because the nose and tongue act as the censors for the proper food intake of the body. If these censors become corrupted by civilization or by any other manifestations, disease ensues (accidents here are excluded). There are three reasons for imbalance or disease:

1. Wrong use of food (wrong combinations)
2. Too much food (overuse)
3. Too little food (insufficiency)

The six tastes differ in function and thus differ from one another in the quality and quantity of their composition, but all contain the constituents of the five elements vital to life: water, air, fire, ether, and earth. According to the Ayurvedas, each taste is formed with two of the five elements predominating; and thus the six tastes differ because they vary in the quality and quantity of their composition of the five elements. The tastes classify the foods as follows:

1. Hot foods are under the element of fire or oxidation and are controlled by the circulatory system. Pungent is hot; Sour is hotter; and Salt is the hottest.

2. Cold foods are under the element of water and are controlled by the lymphatic system, Bitter is cold; Astringent, colder; Sweet, the coldest.
3. Air foods, being projections of the element air, are neither hot nor cold, but they affect the cerebro-spinal system.

These six are all necessary for the body in proper proportions. An increase or decrease in one of the tastes affects the others, and the balance changes for better or worse. The cell affects the tissues; the tissues, the organ; the organ, the system; the system, the systems. All are interrelated and yet independent of one another. All have effective balancing mechanisms to maintain their integrity.

Foods contain one or more of the three elements—Fire, Water and Air—vital to life and naturally those foods containing the three are better than those foods containing only one element. But all foods taken into the body must be balanced in the over-all picture of man. Otherwise the equilibrium is upset and disease ensues. Modern nutrition fails to stress the vibratory rates of foods, the purity and their composition—all of which are affected by fertilizers, planets, and the time of the year. An apple that is grown in the proper environment has an effect on the body that is different from that an apple grown in a poor environment. This accounts for malnutrition in the United States today although the proper (?) foods are eaten. They have not been grown in proper colors (This is not a book on nutrition so that detailed analysis is not called for here).

One concludes that all foods affected by the elements are taken into the body where the tastes play their role as radar signalizers. Outside the body, the foods are affected by the positions of the planets, the time of the year, and the hemisphere in which they are grown. One must never forget that foods have polarity.

Food tables are provided to show the interrelationship of the various elements, the tastes, the planets, the cosmic influences and the color vibrations.

Table 1 lists foods and their color equivalents.

Table 2 lists the metals, chemicals, and their color equivalents.

Table 3 lists foods according to their elements.

Tables 4 A and B provide a list derived from the Chinese, but applied to the northern hemisphere and utilizing the theory of the negative and positive vibrations, the Yin and Yang forces—as the feminine and masculine equivalents. It shows several aspects of Chinese methodology and its awareness of color and cosmic vibrations.

a) Yin is characterized by the colors blue, indigo, purple, green, and white.

b) Yang is characterized by the colors red, orange, brown, yellow and black.

Tables 5 A and B provide an astrological chart with Indian interpretation of time, planetary positions and the signs of the Zodiac as they affect food and color.

Table 6 is a Montage compiled by the author to indicate the role played by the tastes and the elements in disease and the Western equivalents.

Table 1.

Foods and Their Color Equivalents.

Red	Yellow	Blue
Beets	Apricots	Blueberries
Cabbage	Beans	Blue-Skinned Fruits
Cherries	Butter	and Vegetables
Eggplant	Carrots	Grapes
Grapes	Cantaloupe	Plums
Meat	Corn	**Orange**
Onions	Grapefruit	Carrots
Peppers	Lemon	Orange-Skinned Fruits
Radishes	Mangoes	and Vegetables
Red-Skinned Fruits	Melon	Pumpkins
and Vegetables	Onion	Rutabaga
Strawberries	Orange	**Green**
Tomatoes	Papaya	Vegetables and Fruits
Watercress	Peach	of that color
Watermelon	Persimmon	
Yams	Squash	
	Tangerines	
	Turnips	
	Yolk of egg	

Table 2.

Metals, Chemicals, and Their Color Equivalents
(Narrow band of frequency is best)

Red	Green	Blue
Alkaline, various	Aluminum	Aluminum
Barium	Barium	Barium
Bismuth	Carbon	Cadmium
Cadmium	Chlorophyll	Chloroform
Copper	Chlorine	Cobalt
Nitrogen	Chromium	Copper
Iron	Cobalt	Copper Sulphate
Krypton	Copper	Lead
Neon	Ferrous Sulphate	Manganese
Oxygen	Hydrochloric Acid	Nickel
Potassium	Nickel	Oxygen
Rubidium	Nitrogen	Phosphoric Acid
Strontium	Platinum	Tannic Acid
Titanium	Sodium	Titanium
Zinc	Radium	Tin
Orange	Titanium	Zinc
Alkalines (many)	**Indigo**	**Violet**
Aluminum	Bismuth	Aluminum
Antimony	Bromide	Arsenic
Arsenic	Chloral Hydrate	Barium
Boron	Chromium	Calcium
Calcium	Copper	Cobalt
Carbon	Iron	Iron
Copper	Lead	Manganese
Hydrogen	Potassium	Niton (Radon)
Iron	Strontium	Rubidium
Manganese	Titanium	Silver Chloride
Nickel	**Lemon**	Strontium
Rubidium	Citrium	Titanium
Silenium(?)	Germanium	**Purple**
Yellow	Gold	Bromine
Irridium	Iodine	Europium
Magnesium	Iron	Gadolinium
Molybdenum	Phosphorus	Terbium
Platinum	Silver	**Turquoise**
Rhenium	Sulphur	Chromium

Sodium	Thorium	Columbium (Niobium)
Tin	Titanium	Fluorine
Tungsten	Uranium	Mercury
Magenta		Zinc
Irenium		
Lithium		
Potassium		
Rubidium		
Strontium		

Table 3-A

Foods Listed according to Their Elements

Foods should be classified according to their basic elements and used as the needs of the individual dictate. In a country which is hot, the staple food should be rice because it contains water; in a country which is cold, it should be wheat because it contains fire. Listed below are the foods broken down into the three elements: Air, Fire, and Water

Air	Fire	Water
Apples	Celery	Artichoke
Biscuit	Chocolate	Cabbage
Cornflakes	Clover	Cauliflower
Cornmeal	Coffee	Dandelion
Nutmeg	Condiments	Grapefruit
Parsley	Curds	Honey
Salt	Mint	Kelp
Squash	Onion	Lemon
Tea	Parsnip	Lettuce
	Peanuts	Meat
	Peas	Milk
	Pickles	Mushrooms
	Potatoes	Pears
	Pulse	Rice
	Soyabeans	Spinach
	Sugar-Raw	Tomatoes
	Sunflower Seed	Turnip
	Vinegar	Vegetables-all
	Walnut	Water
	Wheat	

Combination of Foods

Air and Fire		Air, Fire, and Water[1]
Bananas	Cream cheese	Black pepper
Beets	Eggs	Cream
Black olives	Endives	Fish
Carrots	Grapes	Garlic
Cream cheese	Oatmeal	Milk
Chestnuts	Yellow corn	

Table 3-B

Diseases and the Elements

DISEASES OF AIR	DISEASES OF FIRE	DISEASES OF WATER
Convulsion	Burning sensation of	Diseases of
Cracking of skin,	the body	Circulation
nails, hair	Digestive diseases	Debilitation
Dwarfism	Hunger — excessive	Digestion
Ear — all diseases	Jaundice	
Eye — all diseases	Odors — foul of body	
Emotional diseases —	Skin diseases	
all	Taste, any unusual	
Fractures of all kinds	kind	
Giddiness	Thirst, excessive	
Headache	Ulcers of any kind	
Hernia		
Hiccough		
Mouth — all diseases		
Neck — wry		
Neuritis of any kind		
Obstruction		
Lock Jaw		
Pain in any part of		
body		
Paralysis of any kind		
Piles		
Shivering		
Skin diseases of any		
kind		
Wry neck		
Yawning		

1. The monks of India and Tibet take seven seeds of black pepper early in the morning and drink some water with it. This keeps them in remarkable shape.

Table 4-A

List of Food Selected by the Chinese and Shown in the Order of Yin to Yang

Devised by Dr. Sakurazawa Ohsawa, **Cours de la Philosophie et de la Medicine d'Extreme-Orient.**

	Cereals		Fish
△	Maize	▽ ▽	Oysters
	Millet		Octopus
	Whole Rice		Eels
	Rye		Carp
	Barley	▽	Hake
	Wheat		Whiting
	Oatmeal		Trout
△ △	Buckwheat		Pike
	Fruits	△	Mussels
			Sole
▽ ▽ ▽	Pineapples	△ △	Salmon
	Grapefruits		Crayfish
	Oranges		Shrimp
	Bananas		Lobster
	Lemons		Herring
	Figs	△ △ △	Sardine
	Pears		
	Grapes		
	Peaches		**Meat**
	Plums		
▽ ▽	Melons	▽	Snails
	Water melons		Frog-legs
	Peanuts		Pork
	Walnuts	△	Hare
▽	Hazel nuts		Rabbit
	Olives, green	△ △	Beef
	Olives, black		Chicken
	Strawberries		Pigeon (Squab)
	Apples		Eggs
△	Chestnuts	△ △ △	Pheasant

Vegetables

▽ ▽ ▽   Tomato
Eggplant
Potatoes
▽ ▽   Pimentoes
Beans
Cucumbers
Asparagus
Peas
Artichokes
String-beans
Beets
Mushrooms
Celery
Red Cabbage
▽   Cauliflower
△   Spinach
Lentils
White Cabbage
Lettuce
Chicory lettuce
Turnip
Radish
Leek
Garlic
Onion
Parsley
Chick peas
Squash, yellow
△ △   Carrots
Salisfy Wat
Water cress
Dandelions, roots
△ △ △   Squash seeds, toasted

Cheeses

▽ ▽   Yoghurt
Little Swiss
▽   Butter Cheese
△   Cream
Milk
△ △   Camembert Cheese
Gruyere
△ △ △   Roquefort

Various Foods

▽ ▽ ▽   Honey
Cooking fats
Cooking oils
Butter
Margarine
▽ ▽   Cocoanut oil
Peanut oil
▽   Sunflower oil
Sesame oil

Beverages

△   Coffee
▽ ▽ ▽   Chocolate
Champagne
Fruit juices
Wine
▽ ▽   Beer
Mineral water
▽   Mineral water without gas
Tea
Herbal Tea
Chicoree
△   Cereal Coffee

Table 4-B

	YANG	YIN
Location	Grows better going north	Grows better going south
Direction of growth	Downward, under-ground	Upward upon the ground
Speed of growth	Slow	Fast
Position on ground	Horizontal	Vertical
Position underground	Vertical	Horizontal
Water	Less	Much required
Cooking time	Long	Short
Grows	Low on ground	High above ground
Change by heat	Hardens	Softens
Color	Red, orange, brown, yellow, black	Green, blue, white, indigo, purple
Sodium Potassium ratio	Less than 5:1	More than 5:1

Table 5-A

India—Astrological Interpretations of Color and Diet

The **Kurma Purana,** which is over fifteen hundred years old, gives an account of the grandfather Creator who is the Maker of Time and is of the Essence of Time. His power is impersonal, omniscient, omnipresent, and his form is made up of an in-numerable variety of rays. Among these rays, the seven rays of the spectrum are the best because they make up the matrices of the seven planets. The sun is the grandfather's deputy for the solar system, and he is given a certain number of cosmic rays for the purpose of creation, maintenance, and destruction of the solar system.

The number of rays varies in accordance with the signs of the Zodiac: Capricorn has 5000 rays; Aquarius, 6000; Sagittarius,

6000; Pisces, 7000; Scorpio, 7000; Aries, 8000; Libra, 8000; Taurus, 9000; Gemini, 10,000; Cancer, 10,000; Virgo, 10,000; Leo, 11,000. This variation in the number of the cosmic rays accounts for changes in climate, season, and temperature and has a strong influence on human behavior.

Astrologers observe that persons born under different signs of the Zodiac are influenced by these rays both prenatally and natally. It is known that the moon affects the tides; so planets do affect our lives. Nutritionists are certain that diet plays an important part in the health of the mother and child. The psychologists know that the emotional state of the mother has an important bearing on the unborn child. Could the explanation be that the position of the sun and planets has an influence upon the color of the foods, which, in turn, influence both mother and child?

The angle of the sun's relationship to the earth affects the light that the plant will receive, the soil, its vitamin and mineral content, as well as the rate of the plant's growth. The food and the amount of sunlight the mother receives naturally affect the child. The tissues if lacking certain of the vitamins, minerals and other foods necessary for their growth—predispose the individual to certain diseases (nutritional) if the conditions are favorable. The rational approach is to balance the deficiency with the proper light and color of the food.

Table 5-B

India—Signs of the Zodiac and Diet Analysis

Aquarius: Jan. 21-Feb. 19; these individuals lack the colors blue and white; they function best by having in their diet fruits and vegetables that are white and blue in color like grapes, pears, honey-dew melons, asparagus, celery, parsnips, potatoes, turnips, fish, chicken, and veal.

Pisces: Feb. 20-March 21; these individuals lack the colors green and white; their most nourishing foods are the root vegetables, tropical fruits and vegetables, fish, chicken, veal, and eggs.

Aries: March 22-April 20; these individuals lack the red rays and need foods rich in that color: peppers, berries, tomatoes, radish, watermelon, cabbage, red meat.

Taurus: April 21-May 21; these individuals lack the yellow rays and are benefited by carrots, melons and turnips. The Taurus individual needs more than the minimal amount of vitamin C and A. He has a tendency to eye trouble.

Gemini: May 22-June 22; these individuals lack the yellow and purple rays; they must eat foods rich in yellow and purple.

Cancer: June 23-July 22; these individuals lack white and green; they thrive best on foods rich in these colors, especially those grown in the shade or in indirect sunlight, such as cucumbers, squash, and melons.

Leo: July 23-Aug. 23; these individuals are deficient in orange and yellow rays; they require more than the normal amount of vitamin C. These individuals do not take the stress of life as easily as others do. Recommended are fruits, melons, pumpkins, squash.

Virgo: Aug. 24-Sep. 23; these individuals lack the violet and gold rays; they need the ripe grains and foods rich in potassium. They have a tendency to tumors and renal diseases and should watch their salt intake.

Libra: Sep. 24-Oct. 23; these individuals lack crimson and gold. They need the fruits and vegetables red and yellow in color especially those that grow above the ground. Meat should be a part of their diet.

Scorpio: Oct. 24-Nov. 22; these individuals lack red and deep scarlet; they require large amounts of liquids, hence they need fruits and vegetables that are watery and are red and yellow in hue. Meat is indicated here. These people have a great deal of nervous energy.

Sagittarius: Nov. 23-Dec. 22; these individuals lack red and gold rays and are usually deficient in enzymes; they need foods rich in the colors red and gold: uncooked foods are beneficial to them.

Capricorn: Dec. 23-Jan. 20; these individuals need the dark green rays; foods rich in dark green hues and the root vegetables are indicated as is food of the sea.

Table 6

Author's Montage: Foods, Elements, Organs, Polarity, Taste, Color and Disease Told in Terms of Western Equivalents.

ORGAN	COLOR	FUNCTION	ELEMENT	POLARITY	
Eyes	Red	Sight	Fire	Positive	— Electron
Tongue	Orange	Taste	Water	Negative	— Proton
Ears*	Blue	Sound	Ether	Neuter	— Neutron
Skin	Violet	Touch	Air	Neuter	— Neutron
Nose	Green	Smell	Earth	Positive	— Electron
Circulation	Yellow	Heat	Fire	Positive	— Subsidiary to Red – Regulates bodily heat
Lymph	Indigo	Sanitation	Water	Negative	— Subsidiary to Orange – Regulates lymph

*All other hollow organs

TASTE (1)	COLOR (2)	ELEMENT	EFFECT ON BODY	MISUSE LEADS TO (3)
Sweet	Green & Orange	Earth & Water	Heat	Obesity, mucous, tumours, fever and glandular swelling
Sour	Green & Red	Earth & Water	Head & Digestion	Eye disease, vertigo, jaundice, ulcers, boils, fever, dropsy and erysipelas
Saline	Orange & Red	Water & Fire	Digestion	Erysipelas, Edema, nephritis, heart trouble
Pungent	Red & Violet	Fire & Air	Digestion Sanitation	Nervous disorders, vertigo
Bitter	Blue & Violet	Ether & Air	Digestion & Sanitation	Diabetes and debilitating diseases
Astringent	Green & Violet	Earth & Air	Sanitation	Debilitating diseases

ELEMENT	FORMS MANIFESTED	Life Force (Prana) Aum Principle:	WESTERN EQUIVALENT OF THE ELEMENTS
Fire	Form, Will	Circulatory System	Carbon Nitrogenoids
Water	Taste, Feeling – pleasure, pain	Lympatic System	Hydrogenoids
Ether	Sound, Intuition	Nervous System	
Air	Touch, Thought	Nervous System	Oxygenoids
Earth	Smell, Consciousness	Energy System	Oxygenoids

Legend: 1. A. Sweet, Sour and Saline are used for air diseases.
   B. Sweet, Bitter and Astringent are used for fire diseases.
   C. Pungent, Bitter and Astringent are used for water diseases.

2. Color is the balancer of all energy. It acts on the sub-atomic and atomic levels, on the ionic and molecular fields, and on the chemical and electrical systems.

3. Disease acts from without-in. Cure takes place from within-out and from cephalic to caudal. Diseases leave the body in reverse order of occurrence—the last disease is first to leave the body.

THE COSMIC CONNECTION

The Hidden Key to Life

The I Ching in the genetic code

by Martin Schonberger

One of the most important discoveries in the history of mankind is that of the genetic code. Every planet as well as all animal life is now recognized as having come into existence, being formed and multiplied by *64 code words* written on the long-chain molecule DNA.

The universal claims of both the I-Ching, "the book of changes," the compendium of Chinese natural knowledge, and the genetic code, "the book of life," encouraged the author to establish the hypothesis of a *general system* in nature. He has verified in numerous parallels the congruence of both the I-Ching code and the genetic code. These sensational results are detailed for the first time in this book.

ISBN 0-88231-023-2

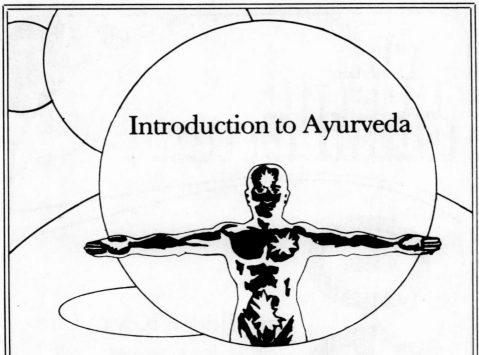

Introduction to Ayurveda

by Dr. Chandrashekhar G. Thakkur

What is Ayurveda? Literally, it means "the Science of Life." (Ayur = Life, Veda = Science.) This traditional Indian system of medicine covers not only the knowledge of life, but the principles of healthy living as well.

As with Acupuncture, the Ayurvedic principles are as useful today as when they were first expounded thousands of years ago; yet they remain largely unknown in the Western world. It is hoped the publication of **INTRODUCTION TO AYURVEDA** will help correct this unfortunate omission.

A PARTIAL LISTING OF CONTENTS INCLUDES:

* The Five Element Theory.
* Anatomy in Ayurveda.
* The Tridosha Theory of Vayu, Pitta and Kapha, which in normal balance sustain health, while their imbalance causes the physical unhappiness known as "Roga" or disease.
* Examination of a patient and principles of treatment.
* Art and Science of Pharmacy. (Indian Herbal Medicine)

ISBN: 0-88231-005-4   Paper 196 pp.

Acupuncture Therapy

by Dr. Mary Austin

This is the most comprehensive textbook of Chinese acupuncture in the English language.

The author, who practices acupuncture and osteopathy, describes in a clear and straightforward manner the complete range of acupuncture techniques, with anatomical references to the structure of the human body.

Dr. Austin presents through text and many detailed illustrations the precise locations of all acupuncture points along the 12 organ meridians (or pathways of energy), as well as the points on the two major vessel meridians. When manipulated by needle, massage, percussion, or Moxa, these points can balance deficiencies and excesses within the body.

ISBN: 0-88231-003-8

(P) EBC   Cloth 276 pp.

The Ear

Gateway to Balancing The Body
A Modern Guide to Ear Acupuncture

by Mario Wexu
D.Ac.

This is the first comprehensive modern textbook of ear acupuncture. The author uniquely combines his extensive personal clinical experience with traditional and modern Chinese and European sources.

Anatomical descriptions with detailed charts clearly illustrate how to locate and use over 300 ear points, both alone and in combination with body points, to treat and prevent illness. Case histories with specific techniques cover treatment of illnesses of the ear itself (deafness, otitis, otalgia), drug and tobacco addiction, alcoholism, obesity, anesthesia, oedema and insomnia.

An excellent repertory listing 150 diseases facilitates an in depth understanding of this incredible and valuable healing art.

ISBN: 0-88231-022-4   Cloth 203 pp.

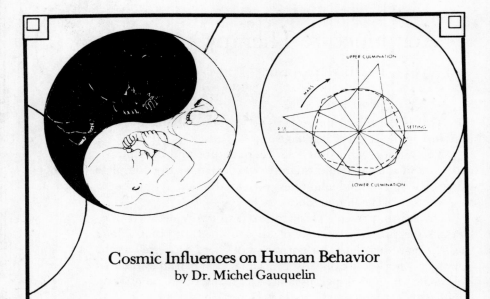

Cosmic Influences on Human Behavior
by Dr. Michel Gauquelin

THE BIRTH HOURS OF WELL-KNOWN SPORT CHAMPIONS.
The circle represents the theoretical findings. The dotted line represents Mars at the birth of 717 ordinary sportsmen. The unbroken line represents Mars at the birth of 2088 champions. The "busy periods" after the rise and culmination are evident.

The astrological hypothesis implies, among other concepts, a relation between vocation and birth horoscopes. Dr. Gauquelin discovered in studying the births of 25,000 European professionals listed in *Who's Who* that certain planets were found more frequently at the rising or culminating positions in the horoscope. For example, Mars ascended or culminated in the case of athletes with the probability against chance distribution ranging from 1 in 50,000 to 1 in 1,000,000!

When first published in 1973, this work was hailed as the most important scientific backing that astrology had ever received. From a strictly scientific viewpoint, Dr. Gauquelin validated the astrological hypothesis: the existence of a correlation between the state of the solar system and the human experience.

This new second edition updates Dr. Gauquelin's research and includes his latest findings on the planetary factors in personality.

Sexual Energy & Yoga

by Elisabeth Haich

The purpose of this book is to introduce the concept of transmuting the physical emotional psychic mental energy people normally disperse in sexual activity for the purpose of uniting their bodies in their higher Self or God. It is hoped that the reader will be open to this information without prejudging it in terms of his personal needs and standards, but just to give a hint of that which is possible. For those readers, who are already aware of this possibility, it is hoped that this book will inspire them.

ISBN: 0-88231-009-7   Paper 160 pp.

THE HEALING ARTS

HOW ATMOSPHERIC CONDITIONS AFFECT YOUR HEALTH

By Dr. Michel Gauquelin

Deaths are more frequent when a weather front passes over. Fogs kill, winds devastate, sudden drops in barometric pressure and electrical agitation in the air affect man—why? and how?

In answering these questions Dr. Gauquelin also postulates the fascinating question of the effect of cosmic influences on our health. Formerly they were not separated from atmospheric conditions. Now, new scientific research reveals the legitimate relationship between the two.

First published in 1971, this new second edition updates the discoveries that have been made since then, about the weather and our health.

Dr. Michel Gauquelin is a Sorbonne trained psychologist and statistician. Since 1969, he has been the director of the *Laboratory for the Study of the Relationship between Cosmic and Psycho-Physicological Rhythms* in Paris, France. An accomplished writer, he is the author of numerous works in the fields of psychology and cosmic science.

ISBN:0-88231-066-6